FORGIVE FORGET FRUITFUL

Turning Offences and Tragedies
into Divine Opportunities

by
John Lewis

**CHI
BOOKS**

CHI–Books
PO Box 6462
Upper Mt Gravatt, Brisbane
QLD 4122
Australia

www.chibooks.org
publisher@chibooks.org

Forgive Forget Fruitful
Turning Offences and Tragedies into Divine Opportunities
Copyright © 2016 by John Lewis

Print ISBN: 978-0-9942607-6-5
eBook ISBN: 978-0-9942607-7-2

Printed in Australia, United Kingdom and the United States of America. Distributed in the USA and Internationally by Ingram Book Group and Amazon. Also available from: Bookdeposity.co.uk and others like Koorong.com in Australia.

Distribution of eBook version: Amazon Kindle, Apple iBooks, Koorong.com and others like Barnes & Nobel NOOK and KOBO.

Cover design: Dave Stone
Layout: Jonathan Gould

What others are saying about this book...

"I wish I could say there is no need for this book in the church. I cannot. The beauty and benefit of forgiveness seems to have been lost. Many have become experts in avoiding the problem or the people who have caused hurt, but while this may feel like healing it never gets to the root of the problem. Rev. John Lewis does not skirt around the issue, but carefully pre-sets the Scriptural basis for forgiveness and the profound fruitfulness that can result.

I encourage everyone to read this book and find the healing that has been freely made available for us through Jesus."

Rev. Dr Lex Akers
Senior Pastor, Hills Wesleyan Church;
District Superintendent, NSW District of the WMC

"After 45 years in Christian ministry, I know too well the truth of a huge number of people who are hurt and offended in church life or in their personal life. I often grieve their pain and loss and pray for their healing and return. In *Forgive Forget Fruitful,* John Lewis addresses the real issues that can see a return to spiritual, emotional and physical health.

This is a must-read book for those who have been hurt and offended and those who reach out to them, as well as those of us who may have caused the hurt or offence."

James Condon
Commissioner, Territorial Commander,
The Salvation Army – Australia Eastern Territory

"This book is a must read for everyone especially Christians. We live tortured lives when we can't forgive because we can't forget all the hurts in our lives. HURTS inflicted by others or brought on by ourselves will render us FRUITLESS and a fruitless life is useless. Please read and be FREE!"

Rev. Robert Lim
Founding Pastor, Evangel Family Church, Singapore;
former Assistant Superintendent of Assemblies of God Singapore

Contents

Foreword

John Lewis has been a mentor and friend to me from the time I entered full time ministry over 30 years ago. He has an incredible passion for the Church and fellow Pastors. With many years as a Senior Pastor of a large church and, more recently, a mentor of pastors, John has a wealth of experience in assisting people navigate the realities of life.

His book, *Forgive Forget Fruitful,* outlines practical application to Biblical principles, particularly in the area of handling offence, hurt and tragedy. The reality of life is that we all go through difficult times that we didn't ask for or even imagine would ever happen to us. We can choose to be either a victim or an overcomer. Combining Biblical truth, life experience and personal research, John outlines a necessary process of moving through those negative experiences to a place of freedom where we recapture the purpose God always intended.

In Matthew 6:9-13 Jesus gave us a magnificent pattern to follow, when we come before 'our Father in Heaven' in prayer. It included praise and petition, along with a cry, 'forgive us...as we forgive others'. The point is clear. We have an obligation – if we live under the Father's forgiveness, we have to live out His forgiveness.

As you read through the following pages, you will discover great insight and your journey will not only take you to a place of wholeness but will also equip and empower you to walk this path with others. You will be inspired to look at difficult situations as opportunities to grow in your relationship with God and others.

This book is a great resource as you embark on your own study on forgiveness.

Wayne Alcorn
National President, Australian Christian Churches

Introduction

This book was birthed out of my concern for the huge number of people that I know personally and others I observe that have been hurt and offended in life generally and in church life specifically. Unfortunately too many of them continue to carry those offences and the consequence has long-term detrimental effects upon their future happiness, wellbeing and destiny.

Drawing from the life of Joseph, we can learn some valuable lessons in dealing with hurts and offences in life. Because of his brothers' brutal and pitiless mistreatment of him, Joseph had every reason to become deeply offended and consumed with anger, bitterness and revenge. Yet Joseph chose to conduct himself from a Godly, rather than a hateful perspective. This perspective was a threefold principle that would not only protect him from a path of cynical revenge, but rather it would empower him to fulfil his Godly destination.

This threefold principle in Joseph's life I call "a trilogy of forgive, forget and fruitful." This trilogy not only brought Joseph through the most inequitable circumstances of his life, but in fact caused him to triumph throughout these tragic events. Joseph was more than just a survivor; he eventually became a recipient of God's double blessing, in family, financially and in National influence. This culminated in him being elevated to the Prime Minister of Egypt.

The application of this "Joseph's trilogy" is such an important factor and so applicable when faced with the realities of endeavouring to live a positive victorious life in the 21st Century. This trilogy if understood and worked out in our lives will not only provide a pathway to spiritual, emotional and physical health, but will also provide a protection from the destructive offences we all confront on our Christian journey.

The key premise behind writing this book is very practical. It is based upon the fact that in life, we all experience offences, overcoming them is an essential challenge for all of us. I know Pastors who have left the ministry because of criticism and conflict with their church leaders. Dr P. Hughes, a highly respected Australian researcher writes that one third of the Australian Pentecostal Pastors leave the ministry because of conflicts with lay leaders.[1]

1. That is a huge number of offended Pastors and lay leaders. George Barna in his book *Revolution* points out that 20 Million American Christians have left the church because they are tired of playing religious games and want more reality.[2] Barna points out these revolutionaries are walking away from church because of their objection to significant issues such as; worship without God's presence, leaders who seek popularity rather than proclaiming truth and leaders who are more concerned about their own legacy than that of Christ. Although Barna does not use the word offended to describe these people, I consider it an appropriate description as to why these revolutionaries refuse to tolerate these perceived unacceptable behaviors, behaviors contradictory to an authentic Christ-like church. I'm calling those people – offended by Church religiously.

2. Specifically I was concerned at the disproportionate attrition rate of Christians leaving the church because they are hurt or offended. Writing for the Schaeffer Institute, Dr. Richard Krejcir, pastor, researcher and author of *The New Exodus; why people leave the Church and how to invite them back,* notes; "every year 2.7 million church members fall into inactivity; this translates into the realisation that a significant percentage of people are leaving the church each

year. From our research, we have found that high percentages are leaving as hurting and wounded victims of some kind of abuse, disillusionment or just plain neglect!" [3]

3. A further study conducted by George Barna among unchurched adults shows that nearly four out of ten non-church going Americans (37%) said they avoid churches because of the negative past experiences in church or with church people.

4. David Huskey estimates 66% of Christians leave the church because they are offended.[4] This is a serious issue that affects not only the individual Christian, but obviously the negative impact upon the momentum of the church to be a vibrant, Christlike influence in the community. In order to put this book in perspective, I readily acknowledge there are numerous reasons people leave the Church. One example is research indicates that the friendliness of a church is a major factor in determining people joining or leaving a church. Clearly there are numerous other reasons people leave the church, however offences are certainly up there with the major contributing factors.

The second reason for this book is theological and deductive, based on what the Bible teaches generally, and what Jesus taught specifically on forgiveness. Forgiveness is an integral part of the Christian doctrine and essential to understanding the Kingdom of God. It is a path to godliness, inner health, peace and happiness. Joseph is an excellent example of the benefits apportioned to those who live a life of forgiveness.

Ethicist Michael Josephson, a former lawyer, law professor, speaker and consultant states, "Whatever your religious views, psychologists say the ability to forgive is closely correlated to happiness." [5] This is further supported by Joshua Loth Liebman who wrote, "We achieve inner health only through forgiveness – the forgiveness is not only of others, but of ourselves." [6]

Studying the life of Joseph demonstrates that forgiveness provides a hope of healing from our past hurts and offences. God in fact can transform major offences into the most powerful and authentic ministry opportunity and influence. And that can result in blessings and benefits, not only for you but toward others and ultimately for the glory of God. This is illustrated uniquely in the account of Joseph and his life experience is the framework for this book. The principles of forgive, forget, and fruitful are not restricted to church life only, but are applicable in life generally for all humanity who are prepared to exercise forgiveness.

1. Dr Philip J Hughes, *The Pentecostals in Australia*, Australian Government Publishing Service, 1996, p.105
2. George Barna, *Revolution*, Tyndale House Publishers, Illinois U.S.A. 2005, p. 13-14
3. Dr Richard Krejcir, Statistics and Reasons for Church Decline – www.churchleadership.org/apps/articles/default.asp?articleid=42346&columnid=4545
4. David Huskey, Fixing the #1 Reason Why People Leave Churches. Tony Cooke Ministries – www.tonycooke.org/articles-by-others/people_leave_churches/
5. Michael Josephson – Forgiveness without condoning or forgetting. A Gift of Inspiration – www.agiftofinspiration.com.au/stories/inspirational/Forgiving.shtml
6. Joseph Loth Liebman, http://thinkexist.com/quotation/we_achieve_inner_health_only_through_forgiveness/196430.html

1

Life Has Many and Varied Offences and Hurts

In this godless world you will continue to experience difficulties. But take heart! I've conquered the world (John 16:33 The Message).

The story of Joseph, is about a man who experienced many and varied hurts, difficulties and offences in his life. Yet in God's perfect timing he fulfils God's purpose in his life (Genesis chs. 37, 39, 40 to the end of Genesis).

The early part of Joseph's life appears to be one drama after another — in his family, workplace and the many events of life that bring hurts and offences. His story would make the television Soap Opera, "Days of our Lives," look rather tame.

We can clearly identify a number of offences and the varying degrees of hurt in each event in Joseph's life, commencing with Israel his father loving Joseph more than his brothers and unwisely demonstrating his favouritism by giving Joseph a very special coat. *"Now Israel loved Joseph more than any of his other sons, because he had been born to him in his old age; and he made a richly ornamented robe for him"* (Genesis 37:3). This became such an offence to his brothers that it caused them to hate him. But when his brothers saw that their father loved him more than all his brothers, they hated him, and could not speak peaceably to him. (Genesis 37:4) Joseph further inflamed the family conflict by acting as a whistle blower to his Dad against his brothers. *"This is the account of Jacob. Joseph, a young man of seventeen, was tending the flocks with his brothers, the sons of Bilhah and the sons of Zilpah, his father's wives, and he brought their father a bad report about them"* (Genesis 37:2). Joseph caused further offence, first to his brothers, then to his parents by suggesting they would all one day bow before him.

Joseph had a dream, and when he told it to his brothers, they hated him all the more. He said to them, "Listen to this dream I had: We were binding sheaves of corn out in the field when suddenly my sheaf rose and stood upright, while your sheaves gathered round mine and bowed down to it." His brothers said to him, "Do you intend to reign over us? Will you actually rule us?" And they hated him all the more because of his dream and what he had said. Then he had another dream, and he told it to his brothers. "Listen," he said, "I had another dream, and this time the sun and moon and eleven stars were bowing down to me." When he told his father as well as his brothers, his father rebuked him and said, "What is this dream you had? Will your mother and I and your brothers actually come and bow down to the ground before you?" His brothers were jealous of him, but his father kept the matter in mind (Genesis 37:5-11).

If only Joseph had read Dale Carnegie's book on "How to win friends and influence people." Maybe he could have influenced them instead of offending them. This young man is like a magnet when it comes to attracting offences.

His brothers retaliate with a momentous offence imposed upon Joseph by first planning to abandon him in a pit to die. Eventually they come to a decision to sell him to some Midianite traders who are heading to Egypt. (Genesis 37: 19-28) His brothers then offended their father by deceitfully insinuating Joseph had been eaten by a wild animal. *"He recognised it and said, "It is my son's robe! Some ferocious animal has devoured him. Joseph has surely been torn to pieces"* (Genesis 37:33). This was a deep and perpetual hurt in Israel's life (v.35).

This story of intrigue and offence in the life of Joseph and his family continues to follow him into Egypt. There Potiphar's wife accuses Joseph of attempting to rape her, although a total fabrication, he was still thrown in jail. (Genesis 39) He experiences another offence when after interpreting the cupbearer's dream; the cupbearer forgot to mention Joseph's plight to Pharaoh, as Joseph had requested him. *"Yet the chief butler did not remember Joseph, but forgot him"* (Genesis 40:23).

OFFENCES OCCUR IN EVERY DAY LIFE

I am sure we all know business owners, Chief Executive Officer's, bosses and managers who have been offended by members of their staff who started their own business in competition with, and in close proximity to their present employer.

I empathise with those Senior Pastors who have been offended by Pastors and leaders on their ministry team who have started another church in the same geographical area without the approval of the Senior Pastor. They have attracted people to join with them at considerable cost financially and numerically to that Senior Pastor, and the negative impact on that Church. Having held a National Executive role in the movement to which I belong, I know this occurs far too frequently.

I am aware of the well–meaning but somewhat trite and crude response offered to Senior Pastors such as "Suck it up and get on with life." I can only assume this insensitive advice is an attempt to prevent the offended Pastor from becoming obsessed with bitterness. I doubt the advice is a soothing balm to the raw emotions being experienced by the offended Pastor. It is hardly a Biblical solution to a painful offence that happens far too often, as I have experienced personally.

Without appearing callous and indifferent, I am sure there are a number of people who are supersensitive and become offended over insignificant, petty, non–issues. A good dose of maturity would solve the majority of their problems.

> No one is immune from the fact that life can appear to be unfair, confusing and even cruel, and bad things do happen to good people.

My research and life experience in the ministry has taught me that no one is immune from the fact that life can appear to be unfair, confusing and even cruel, and bad things do happen to good people. It is a fact that sometimes beautiful, godly people appear to die prematurely and that babies and children can be the innocent victims of sickness, disease and even death. I quit trying long ago to explain the unexplainable as to why these things happen on life's journey. I now endeavour to look for the evidence of God's grace empowering those, who when confronted by such grief, offences, or tragedies, will eventually (for there will be a time frame), display grace to reach out and minister to others who are going through similar circumstances on their journey.

Hopefully this book will provide a Biblical process that enables you to face the hurts, offences and even tragedies that often make up the realities of life, with a sense of purpose that empowers you to get beyond any sense of the victim status, and to see how God can turn the negative past into a positive future. The Oxford dictionary defines victimisation as –'to make a victim of, to single out (a person) to suffer ill treatment.' When we consider ourselves as victims we become helpless and have the sense of no control over our lives and often we reject help. Unfortunately it is a path of self-pity that leads to depression and may end in suicide. John Gardner writes "Self-pity is easily the most destructive of the non-pharmaceutical narcotics: it is addictive, gives momentary pleasure and separates the victim from reality."[1] Apparently Joseph never yielded to the deadly temptation of self-pity. There is a powerful Biblical theme that strength can emerge out of our weakness, that hope can break through the barrier of hopelessness and that tragedy can lead to triumph. The narrative of Joseph's life is one of triumphing over hurts and offences that can eventually lead to God's ultimate purpose and blessing. There are numerous scriptures confirming this principle such as:

And the God of all grace, who called you to his eternal glory in Christ, after you have suffered a little while, will himself restore you and make you strong, firm and steadfast (1 Peter 5:10).

It is so easy for us to quote such scriptures as the above and include that very well known verse in Romans 8:28 – *"And we know that in all things*

God works for the good of those who love Him, who have been called according to His purpose." The problem arises in applying that truth when we are going through deep waters.

I trust the lessons learned from Joseph may assist to increase your faith that Christ's lordship is in every area of our life – the good, the bad and the ugly.

1. John Gardner, www.goodreads.com/quotes/429997-self-pity-is-easily-the-most-destructive-of-the-non-pharmaceutical

fff

2

Facing the Facts –
Offences Will Come

"An unexamined life is not worth living." Socrates.

The proposition that it is impossible to avoid offences necessitates the approach of not endeavouring to avoid offences, but rather how can we deal with offences that come our way. And how can I transform offences into maturing benefits in my life and to the advancement of God's Kingdom – it is indeed a great challenge with exciting prospects.

UNDERSTANDING THE REALITY OF OFFENCES

The definition of offence: "The act of creating resentful hurt feelings, displeasure. The condition of being offended, especially of feeling hurt, resentful or angry." Webster's Dictionary.

The Free Dictionary definition: "A violation or infraction of a moral or social code: a transgression or sin."

Offences can range from simple perceptions such as being misunderstood, undervalued, overlooked, to being insulted, imposed upon, unfairly treated, deep

> Learning to handle small offences can be good lessons and a great preparation for handling the major offences in life.

ongoing or unresolved conflicts, to be lied about, a target for innuendos and character assassination. On a physical level there is emotional and sexual abuse, cruelty, torture and even death.

The range in my definition is intended to be comprehensive because I think there are various levels of offence. Tragedies and offences in life span an enormous scope. Yet learning to handle small offences can be good lessons and a great preparation for handling the major offences in life.

PHYSICAL ABUSE IS OFFENSIVE

We should not underestimate the magnitude of offence perpetrated by acts of violence whether between neighbours, in the work place, the result of road rage, at parties, pubs, sports events, the list is endless. One of the most concerning aspects of offences is evident in the increase of domestic violence. Current figures in Australian show that 23% of woman who had never been married in common law (*de-facto* relationship), experienced violence by a partner at some time during the relationship. 42% of woman who had been in previous relationship reported violence by a previous partner. Half of women experiencing violence by their current partner experienced more than one incident of violence. Injuries sustained in the last incident were mainly bruising, cuts, scratches, but also can included stabs, or gunshot wounds, and other injuries. 35% experienced violence from their partner during periods of separation.[1] Research indicates domestic violence occurs toward both males and females.[2] We have not included a separate identification of sexual violence or the disturbing number of incidences of teenage dating violence including the physical, emotional and sexual abuse of young teens.

This book is not about violence, these statistics above simply provide examples to indicate the extent to which so many people are abused and offended, and the need for assistance in recovery. I was recently talking with a lady who is a professional worker with children and she said she would cry when reading some of the reports of the inhumane treatment children can receive in their own homes.

JESUS WARNED OF THE INEVITABILITY OF OFFENCES

Then He said to the disciples, "It is impossible that no offences should come, but woe to him through whom they do come! It would be better for him if a millstone were hung around his neck, and he were thrown into the sea, than that he should offend one of these little ones" (Luke 17: 1-2 NKJV).

Paraphrasing what Jesus is saying and applying it to modern 21st century life, – "If you have never been offended, hurt or wounded – you are either incredibly tough, or unaware of what is happening to you, or you are insulated from life, or you are from another planet." Offences are a fact of life according to Jesus.

When Jesus uses the word impossible in relation to offences, He uses the Greek verb (anendekton) which means to admit to oneself the "inadmissible or unavoidable" [3] He is stating it is an impossible or unavoidable fact of life that hurts will come. The denial of that fact is unhealthy, unrealistic and poor theology.

The word offence in the Greek is Skandala from which we derive the English word scandal. The Complete Biblical Library Commentary notes that the word scandal corresponds to the Hebrew word "Yaquash" which means, "to catch in a trap, or snare." Another Hebrew derivative is Kasal, which means, "to stumble." Over time these two words emerged into one, resulting in meaning "the cause of ruin, a stumbling block." [4] It is obvious therefore offences would be one of the weapons the enemy would use to trap, snare, and to stumble the saints. Lenski in his Commentary points out the word offence "goes beyond the idea of stumbling (from which one may recover) and always denotes Spiritual destruction. [5] The Complete Biblical Library suggests "offence" carries the strong connotation of "cause to reject God." [6]

That has to be one of the great tragedies in the modern Christian Church that so many people become trapped, snared and stumble to the point of their spiritual destruction. Unfortunately so many will discontinue their church attendance and many will quit following the Lord. Others may continue to attend church, but their unresolved offence and bitterness will prevent their maturity and being fully released in their God given ministry potential.

It is essential therefore; we understand that offences are inevitable and unavoidable, so awareness and preparation of heart and attitude can assist in the prevention of deep and lasting negative consequences.

1. Australian Bureau of Statistics on Domestic Violence in Australia, www.abs.gov.au
2. www.oneinthree.com.au/overview
3. Fritz Rienecker/Cleon Rogers, *Linguistic Key to the Greek New Testament*, Zondervan Publishing House, Grand Rapids, U.S.A. p. 191
4. Executive Editor Ralph W. Harris, *The Complete Biblical Library Volume 4 Luke*, The Complete Biblical Library, Springfield Missouri, U.S.A. 1988, p. 503
5. Ralph Earle, *Beacons Biblical Library Volume 6 Matthew. Mark. Luke.* Beacon Hill Press, Kansas City Missouri, U.S.A. 1964, p. 169
6. Executive Editor Ralph W. Harris, *The Complete Biblical Library Volume 4 Luke*, The Complete Biblical Library, Springfield Missouri, U.S.A. 1988, p. 503

3

Offences in the Church
are a Fact

"For we all often stumble and fall and offend in many things" (James 3:2 Amplified Bible).

Pastor and Church leader David Huskey states 66% of people leave the church because they are offended. That is a very disturbing statistic. It suggests there are a huge percentage of people who are not handling the offences in their lives.[1]

Huskey in fact points out his research indicates it is the number one reason why people leave the Church. It is most unfortunate these offended people will probably take their offences with them to the next church and a percentage will not attend any church. Clearly people being offended is not the only reason they leave church. I have already mentioned the friendship factor that contributes toward people leaving the Church. George Barna in his book *Revolution* estimates there are over twenty million Christians in America that he calls "Revolutionaries," because they are no longer willing to attend churches that lack authenticity. They are disillusioned with the weak, traditional religiosity in the Church. These Revolutionaries no longer attend Church. However many still claim to love God, and maintain a commitment and personal devotion to Christ, but seek their development outside the Church.[2]

DO NOT OFFEND CHRIST'S LITTLE ONES

It would be better for him if a millstone were hung around his neck, and he were thrown into the sea, than that he should offend one of these little ones (Luke 17:2 NKJV).

A millstone necklace does not sound very attractive.

When Jesus uses the word "little ones" some commentators suggest He is not just referring to children, for the word He uses is 'micron' which means small in stature, age, influence, but may also be referring to new converts or those who have a child-like innocence.[3] How tragic to see, young converts offended by supposedly mature Christians who should know better: those pharisaic legalists who bring condemnation on a new Christian for such things as smoking, hair style, or their expected dress code instead of allowing the Holy Spirit time to bring the adjustments as and when He thinks appropriate. These legalists impose their dress and lifestyle preferences on these "little ones" and so often burden them with yokes they cannot bear and by their offences they cause others to stumble. Modern day Pharisees can cause many offences.

NINE POSSIBLE AREAS OF OFFENCE

This is not a comprehensive list but here are some examples:

1. **Doctrinal Offence**

   Paul constantly contended with the Judaizes who wanted to mix the law with Paul's message emphasising faith and grace. e.g. they wanted to include the Old Testament laws such as circumcision, eating of meats, keeping the Sabbath and Holy Days.

   The Spirit clearly says that in later times some will abandon the faith and follow deceiving spirits and things taught by demons. Such teachings come through hypocritical liars, whose consciences have been seared as with a hot iron. They forbid people to marry and order them to abstain from certain foods, which God created to be received with thanksgiving by those who believe and who know the truth. For everything God created is good, and nothing is to be rejected if it is received with thanksgiving, because it is consecrated by the word of God and prayer. If you point these things out to the brothers, you will be a good minister of Christ Jesus, brought up in the truths of the faith and of the good teaching that you have followed. Have nothing to do with godless myths and old wives' tales; rather, train yourself to be godly (1 Timothy 4:1-7).

Too many young converts have been overwhelmed by legalistic regulations and church traditions that are man imposed and not biblical requirements.

> Too many young Christians have walked away from God because of the apparent contradicting life style of a seemingly more mature Christian.

2. **Doubting God's Word**

   Satan's initial offence with Adam and Eve was to cast doubt on God's Word *"Has God said?"* (Genesis 3:1). Beware of those who cast doubt on God's Word: the super cynic who doubts the supernatural intervention of God and those who hold a cessationist theology and relegate the supernatural work and manifestations of the Holy Spirit to the first century church. These people can be in the church – not just rank atheists.

3. **Poor theology that produces unrealistic expectations**

   Some extremes of the faith teaching fail to account for the "sovereignty of the God" factor which can produce an arrogant demand on God performing what they believe is their Biblical promise and authority; this can lead to disillusionment and a collapse of faith. Unfortunately for them they learn the hard way that God is still God and He will not be intimidated. This must be balanced with the biblical instruction to pray and believe that our God is the God of the supernatural.

4. **Contradictory Life Style**

Paul instructs Timothy to be a godly example in speech, life, love, faith and purity. *"Don't let anyone look down on you because you are young, but set an example for the believers in speech, in life, in love, in faith and in purity"* (1 Timothy 4:12).

Too many young Christians have walked away from God because of the apparent contradicting life style of a seemingly more mature Christian. I know of Pastors who have walked away from the ministry because of the contradictory behavior of other Pastors. I know of a young Pastor who no longer attends church because of the inappropriate behavior of his Senior Pastor in relationship to excessive alcohol.

5. **Leading Others Astray**

What a tragedy to see a young person led astray by friendships at school, or even worse, when led astray by another friend in the Church or Youth group, exposing them to sex, drugs, and alcohol, etc.

6. **Deceptive Business Deals**

This becomes apparent when a professing Christian conducts business in a questionable manner. Where spin replaces truth and deception is an acceptable practice. The lack of Christian ethics leads to confusion in a young convert's mind, especially those who are desirous of living a godly life.

7. **Inappropriate Behaviour**

By leaders and clergy in such areas as sexual and verbal abuse, hurtful and abusive attitudes, control freaks, bullying, manipulating people, those who should know better and they gossip, destroying by innuendos. May God have mercy on them!

8. **Relationship Breakdown**

Inside and outside the Church, divorce, broken engagements, parting of friendships, and family feuds. These can lead to offences that cause some people to blame God and walk away from the Church.

9. **Victims of physical, sexual, emotional abuse**

Be that in family, relatives, close friends or strangers, the offence is traumatic. During the recent Royal Commission appointed to investigate institutional sexual abuse of children in Australia, the nation was shocked at the magnitude of sexual abuse that has taken place in religious institutions and the failure to deal appropriately with the offenders and more disconcerting the offended.

My prayer – "Heavenly Father, pour out your grace and the ability to forgive on those who have been offended and abused by Clergy, leaders, and congregations in your church, especially those little ones who have become offended, disillusioned, and disengaged with You because of the offences against them. Graciously bring healing and restore them we pray, Amen."

1. David Huskey, Fixing the #1 Reason Why People Leave Churches. Tony Cooke Ministries – www. tonycooke.org/articles-by-others/people_leave_churches/
2. George Barna, *Revolution*, Tyndale House Publishers, Inc, Illinois U.S.A. 2005, p. 13
3. Ralph Earle, *Beacons Biblical Library Volume 6 Matthew. Mark. Luke.* Beacon Hill Press, Kansas City Missouri U.S.A. 1964, **p. 169**

fff

4

Forgiveness – A Path of Hope

Hebrews 11:1 *"Now faith is being sure of what we hope for…"* The foundation of the Christian faith is based on hope.

"A leader is a dealer in hope." Napoleon Bonaparte.

When Joseph forgave and reunited with his brothers, he expressed a hope of his whole family reuniting especially with his elderly father.

Clearly life generally and the Christian life specifically cannot guarantee anybody a bulletproof protection from the offences of living on planet earth. Jesus made that abundantly clear. The good news is God has provided for us a path of dealing with these offences called forgiveness; that should we choose to embark upon that path, it can lead to blessing and fruitfulness. Following that path of forgiveness also provides an understanding that God can turn our past offences into opportunities for God's glory. This Christian perspective will protect us from a sense of unfairness, bitterness and victimisation, and provides a living hope for the future.

MY PERSONAL EXPERIENCE IN FORGIVENESS IN MY EARLY DAYS OF MINISTRY

I was a Youth Leader in my early twenties in a large church in Victoria. I was impressed by the great work David Wilkerson of Teen Challenge from the U.S.A. He was effectively reaching street kids in the ghettos of New York. So we decided to commence a coffee shop outreach. We hired a Church hall for Friday and Saturday nights – redecorated it to attract the 'youth and the teen' generation. It was a dimly lit atmosphere, candlelights, special menus, our youth dressed up as waiters, background music playing and a great atmosphere.

My senior Pastor attended one Saturday night and I anticipated he would have been delighted that we had so many unchurched kids in the Coffee shop, and many were getting saved each week.

My hopes were dashed when during the following Sunday morning service my Senior Pastor began criticising our outreach publically; stating we were copying the world and God would not bless such an activity. I was fuming during the service and unable to contain my anger, I stormed up to my Pastor after the meeting and demanded to see him in his office. I proceeded to berate him for his cowardly act of criticising me publically instead of correcting me privately. I then stormed out and slammed the door behind me. The next few weeks were hell on earth for me in church, I was still fuming to the point of imagining what damage a fit young twenty-three year old could impose on this very small of stature elderly Senior Pastor.

One Sunday evening we were singing our closing hymn and I believe the Holy Spirit clearly told me to apologise and seek forgiveness from my Senior Pastor. I tried the old debate trick of defending myself and pointing out he should apologise to me, as he had caused the offence, he should know better and I at least obeyed the Biblical injunction of going to my brother privately and expressing my grievance. The Holy Spirit's insistence would not recede, nor could I ignore the reality of His impression on my heart.

> The great lesson is forgiveness lights the pathway of hope and restoration.

I eventually made my way to the altar of the church where he was still praying for a few people. At the appropriate time I approached him and asked for his forgiveness for my obnoxious behaviour towards him. He kissed me on the cheek and prayed what I realised afterwards was a powerful prophetic prayer. I cannot recall ALL of his prayer but one sentence was indelibly printed on my mind "Lord, anoint this young man and send him to the four corners of the world with your Gospel."

Remember this was Sunday evening – on the following Tuesday my Pastor was involved in a head – on car accident, he was in a coma and died not many days later. You can imagine how glad I was for the Holy Spirit's opportunity to make my peace and receive forgiveness before my Pastor passed away.

But here is a major point in my story, I have in fact travelled and preached in over 36 countries of the world. This is my personal experience of ministry fruitfulness emerging from an offence when we handle the offence by appropriating God's way which begins with forgiveness — this I call the fruitfulness that results from obedience: obedience and God's graciousness in fulfilling my Pastor's prophetic prayer. I thank God for the incredible anointing on my Pastor's life and the Godly leadership he provided, what a wonderful privilege to grow up under such a mighty man of God.

The great lesson is forgiveness lights the pathway of hope and restoration.

5

Forgiveness – The First Step to Recovery

"The only unforgivable sin: Being unforgiving." Malcolm Forbes.

Forbes is emphasising the necessity of forgiveness, however we understand Jesus did address the sin of blasphemy against the Holy Spirit as being an unforgivable sin (Matthew 12:31-32).

In Genesis 45 Joseph wept loudly over his brothers. His forgiveness was sincere and unashamed. No doubt his emotional outburst was from a well of deep hurt, yet overwhelmed by deeper emotions called love and true forgiveness. Like the bursting through of a dam wall, Joseph let thirteen years of offence, hurt, maybe bitterness and anger, be released by a river of emotional cleansing of forgiveness.

FORGIVENESS IS ONE OF THE KEY CURRENCIES OF GOD'S KINGDOM

The unique and distinctive teaching of Jesus included His emphasis on forgiveness. It was so contradictory to the revengeful "eye for an eye" teaching of the law (Exodus 21:24) and the philosophy of that day and especially living under a cruel, dominant Roman Empire, that would make forgiveness almost impossible to exercise. Yet the emphasis on forgiveness that was clearly taught by Jesus, and ultimately demonstrated by him when on the cross, reveals to us God's high priority and perspective on forgiveness.

THE SPIRITUAL BENEFITS OF LIVING IN FORGIVENESS

1. **FORGIVENESS IS THE HEART OF THE GOSPEL** – *"In him we have redemption through his blood, the forgiveness of sins, in accordance with the riches of God's grace"* (Ephesians 1:7).

2. **FORGIVENESS IS GOD'S ONGOING CLEANSING POWER** – *"If we confess our sins he is faithful and just and will forgive us our sins and purify us from all unrighteousness."* (1 John 1:9).

3. **FORGIVENESS PREVENTS THE DEVIL'S FOOTHOLD** – *"...and do not give the Devil a foothold"* (Ephesians 4:27), in the context of not letting the sun go down on our anger.

4. **FORGIVENESS PREVENTS US GRIEVING THE HOLY SPIRIT** – *"And do not grieve the Holy Spirit of God, with whom you were sealed for the day of redemption. Get rid of all bitterness, rage and anger, brawling and slander, along with every form of malice. Be kind and compassionate to one another, forgiving each other, just as in Christ God forgave you"* (Ephesians 4:30-32). Paul notes that bitterness, rage, anger, brawling, slander, and malice grieve the Holy Spirit and he then encourages the antidote to those grievances against the Holy Spirit by instructing us to choose to be kind, compassionate, and FORGIVING, as in Christ God forgave us. I doubt there would be a person reading this book who has not grieved the Holy Spirit in some degree of anger, or malice, and yet we so easily omit to resolve that grievance by failing to offer or request forgiveness not only from the person who angered us, but failing to ask the Holy Spirit's forgiveness also. Jesus taught us to pray for forgiveness from our heavenly Father and the willingness of forgiveness we offer to others we will receive from God. *"And forgive us our debts as we forgive our debtors"* (Matthew 6:12).

THE PHYSICAL AND EMOTIONAL BENEFITS IN FORGIVENESS

The Mayo Clinic report on forgiveness is encouraging; forgiveness makes way for compassion, kindness, and peace; healthier relationships, greater spiritual and psychological wellbeing, less stress and hostility. Lowers blood pressure, fewer symptoms of depression; lower risk of alcohol and substance abuse.[1]

Jesus taught we must exercise multiple acts of forgiveness. *"Then Peter came to Him and said, "Lord, how often shall my brother sin against me, and I forgive him? Up to seven times Jesus said to him, "I do not say to you, up to seven times, but up to seventy times seven?"* (Matthew 18:21-22 NKJV).

Peter was looking for some guidelines on the boundaries to this forgiveness teaching Jesus was presenting. Maybe he thought that unlimited acts of forgiveness appeared a little extreme and impractical in terms of real life relationships. Jesus clarifies the issue by explaining to Peter that multiple offences (seventy times seven) of forgiveness were indeed the way of His Kingdom.

Jesus exemplified the greatest act of forgiveness when hanging on the cross, surrounded by those who had put Him there, when He cried out, *"Father forgive them for they know not what they do"* (Luke 23: 34 NKJV). I must admit this scripture has been a little problem for me. For I'm sure they knew exactly what they were doing. I can only assume Jesus implied that they did not understand the full eternal ramification in crucifying Him. Paul on a number of occasions taught on the importance of forgiveness.

Therefore, as God's chosen people, holy and dearly loved, clothe yourselves with compassion, kindness, humility, gentleness and patience. Bear with each other and forgive whatever grievances you may have against one another. Forgive as the Lord forgave you. And over all these virtues put on love, which binds them all together in perfect unity. Let the peace of Christ rule in your hearts, since as members of one body you were called to peace. And be thankful (Colossians 3: 12-15).

He instructs the church to "Forgive as the Lord forgave you." Paul understood the oil on troubled waters in church life was forgiveness. He wrote to the church at Philippi that they would be a people "without offence" (Philippians 1:10). Again Paul reinforces what Jesus had stated

> Offences and grievances will come across our path and God's remedy in dealing with them is to choose to forgive.

to his disciples *"that offences are bound to come, but woe to that person through whom they come"* (Luke.17:1). Yet Paul encourages those Christians to live beyond offences. Again he teaches the Colossians *"Bear with each other and forgive whatever grievances you may have against one another"* (Colossians 3:13). Clearly Paul is acknowledging that offences and grievances will come across our path and God's remedy in dealing with them is to choose to forgive.

When Jesus taught his disciples to pray he included *"forgive us our debts as we also have forgiven our debtors"* (Matthew 6:12). It would appear the intended regular application of that prayer included forgiveness; maybe forgiveness should be a regular daily exercise as required.

Lewis B. Smedes identifies the reality of offences and the need to forgive. He writes "Forgiveness is God's invention for coming to terms with a world in which, despite their best intentions, people are unfair to each other, and hurt each other deeply. He began by forgiving us, and He invites us all to forgive each other." [2]

DO NOT POSTPONE FORGIVENESS

Jesus encourages us to act urgently on issues of forgiveness and quickly resolve personal conflicts. *"You have heard that it was said to the people long ago, 'Do not murder, and anyone who murders will be subject to judgment.' But I tell you that anyone who is angry with his brother will be subject to judgment. Again, anyone who says to his brother, 'Raca,' is answerable to the Sanhedrin. But anyone who says, 'You fool!' will be in danger of the fire of hell. "Therefore, if you are offering your gift at the altar and there remember that your brother has something against you, leave your gift there in front of the altar. First go and be reconciled to your brother; then come and offer your gift. "Settle matters quickly with your adversary who is taking you to court. Do it while you are still with him on the way, or he may hand you over to the judge, and the judge may hand you over to the officer, and you may be thrown into prison. I tell you the truth, you will not get out until you have paid the last penny"* (Matthew 5: 21-26).

If you bring an offering to the altar and remember you have an offence with a brother, leave your gift and go make it right with your brother (paraphrased). Jesus instructs us to resolve disagreements and anger in our hearts against our brother and to do so with a sense of urgency, as opposed to hoping it will resolve itself. By leaving the altar and going to that brother and reconciling with him first, we understand the kingdom of God's values and spiritual principles on earth.

This principle of dealing with offences or the misunderstandings that affect our relationships sooner rather than later, is Christ's recommended approach. If acted upon quickly we would resolve so many difficulties in our marriages, business dealings, in the Church, and in relationships generally. Have you ever met some people who cut you off, ignored or avoided you when something comes between you and them? I think that is one of the most difficult situations to handle, and clearly Jesus taught us to get our attitude right and go to that person with a sense of urgency. Realising not everybody finds confrontation easy or pleasant, yet we cannot hide behind any meek disposition and excuse dealing with the issue as Jesus taught us to do so. It is so easy to minimise the effects of the offence by rationalizing to ourselves that time will heal the hurt and we will get over it. When in fact time may cool the initial heated reaction, but not necessarily cleanse the infected emotions, nor remove the barrier preventing openness and transparency toward those who have offended us. Clearly in this chapter Jesus is teaching that forgiveness and where possible, reconciliation is God's path forward into His presence and enjoying true worship when standing at the altar offering your gift (Matthew 5:23). I suggest that maybe failing to obey Christ's resolution to offences may have a chain of consequences that follow. Adam and Eve had a chain of consequences to their disobedience to God's command, such as broken fellowship with God. They were ex-communicated from the garden; it brought sin into the world. As Jesus is addressing bringing our gifts to the altar in the context of forgiveness, maybe our failure to do so has a chain of consequences, such as reduced sensitivity to the Holy Spirit's voice, or a reduced sense of God's presence, or a reduced manifestation of his power. The powerful benefits of forgiveness should not be minimised in the Church today.

Paul supports the urgency of resolving offences in Ephesians 4:26 ... *"Do not let the sun go down while you are still angry."* That is a clear time

> Forgiveness does not make the offence committed right, but forgiveness is God's path to restoration.

frame in which to act on. I must admit that knowing God's urgency to resolve an offence is not always my first and immediate response. Depending on the degree of offence has often determined my willingness and speed to which I resolve the situation. Forgiveness does not make the offence committed right, nor should it convey any trivialising of the offence; but forgiveness is God's path to restoration.

1. www.mayoclinic.org/healthy-lifestyle/adult-health/in-depth/forgiveness/art-20047692

2. Lewis Smedes, www.azquotes.com/quote/523166

fff

6

Lessons From Joseph on How to Implement Forgiveness

"As I walked out of the door towards the gate that would lead to my freedom, I knew if I didn't leave my bitterness and hatred behind, I'd still be in prison." Nelson Mandela.[1]

JOSEPH IS A GREAT MODEL WHEN EXERCISING FORGIVENESS

The book of Genesis devotes fourteen chapters to the story of Joseph and that should indicate the significant value God placed on his life. It is a story highlighting God's sovereignty and how he can turn offences, hurts and tragedy into incredible triumph.

I will spend a considerable portion of this book addressing forgiveness because it is in my opinion, the starting place of restoration for a person who has been offended, and still carries hurt and bitterness. It is futile to address offences and think we can bypass forgiveness. Endeavouring to somehow put offences behind us, refusing to think about it, or maybe we prefer to become preoccupied with other activities, but unfortunately none of these will resolve the offence.

Italian Psychiatrist and founder of Psychosynthesis Dr Robert Assugioli summed it up this way "Without forgiveness life is governed by an endless cycle of resentment and retaliation." [2]

Joseph faces his brothers.

Then Joseph could no longer control himself before all his attendants, and he cried out, "Make everyone leave my presence!" So there was no–one with Joseph when he made himself known to his brothers. And he wept so loudly that the Egyptians heard him, and Pharaoh's household heard about it. Joseph said to his brothers, "I am Joseph! Is my father still living?" But his brothers were not able to answer him, because they were terrified at his presence. Then Joseph said to his brothers, "Come close to me." When they had done so, he said, "I am your brother Joseph, the one you sold into Egypt! And now, do not be distressed and do not be angry with yourselves for selling me here, because it was to save lives that God sent me ahead of you. For two years now there has been famine in the land, and for the next five years there will not be ploughing and reaping. But God sent me ahead of you to preserve for you a remnant on earth and to save your lives by a great deliverance. "So then, it was not you who sent me here, but God. He made me father to Pharaoh, lord of his entire household and ruler of all Egypt" (Genesis. 45:1-8).

He kissed all his brothers and wept over them. Afterwards his brothers talked with him.

Let us consider Joseph's eight – point example on exercising a process of forgiveness.

Although I appreciate this story is set in an ancient culture and the possibility some of the responses expressed by Joseph and his brothers may vary from culture to culture and family to family; however, there are key principles of forgiveness and restoration for all to learn in this remarkable story of Joseph.

1. THE GRACE THAT EMPOWERS FORGIVENESS

Joseph chose to exercise grace towards his brothers. By any due process of law or reasonable measures of justice these brothers did not deserve the grace of forgiveness; they deserved punishment. This grace that empowered Joseph to forgive is powerfully reflected in Christ and His ability to demonstrate forgiveness, in particular when hanging on the cross, and asking the Father to forgive those who put Him there. We are all undeserving of God's grace, His forgiveness and restoration. Just as God chose to forgive, and Joseph also chose to operate out of grace and forgive, so we can also choose to operate out of grace, and forgive.

2. MAKE IT PRIVATE

Joseph cleared the room of all the Egyptians *"...and he cried out, "Make everyone leave my presence!"* (Genesis 45:1). One of the basic principles in the process of negotiating forgiveness and restoration is choosing the correct TIME, PLACE AND CIRCUMSTANCES. It must never be attempted in a flippant, rushed or pessimistic attitude. It requires a preparation of faith, prayer, unrestricted time and uninterrupted privacy.

> When forgiveness is seriously desired, deceit has no place in the negotiation.

3. REVEALED HIMSELF

He made himself known to his brothers. *Then Joseph could no longer control himself before all his attendants, and he cried out, "Make everyone leave my presence!" So there was no–one with Joseph when he made himself known to his brothers"* (Genesis 45:1).

The humility of this Prime Minister of Egypt to relinquish any pride or self-saving egotism and to stand emotionally naked before his brethren for their acceptance or ridicule is truly astonishing. Surely this provides us with an insight into the depth and quality of character regarding this great man Joseph. How commendable, the open and transparent approach regarding his intention, where there were no hidden agendas. When forgiveness is seriously desired, deceit has no place in the negotiation. Transparency is paramount in establishing a communication of trust based on truth. Joseph illustrates the heart of God who humbly displayed His genuine desire for restoration with His great family that He created in His image, by sending Jesus to restore unity with all humanity. Highlighting again Jesus was totally vulnerable and fully transparent, even to his enemies.

4. HE EXPRESSED WARMTH, COMPASSION AND INTIMACY

"...come close to me" (Genesis 45:2-4). Joseph avoided anger or retaliation his goal was to win their trust and confidence regarding his sincerity to

be re-united. His outburst of crying may have made him vulnerable to his brothers but it also exposed his heart to them. In pursuing a path of reconciliation there is a place for expressing a genuine warmth and compassion that can assist in bridging an enormous gap of hostility.

5. HE EXPRESSED GOD'S PURPOSE IN HIS LIFE

God sent me ahead of you to preserve for you a remnant on earth and to save your lives. And now, do not be distressed and do not be angry with yourselves for selling me here, because it was to save lives that God sent me ahead of you. For two years now there has been famine in the land, and for the next five years there will not be ploughing and reaping. But God sent me ahead of you to preserve for you a remnant on earth and to save your lives by a great deliverance (Genesis 45:5-7). Joseph lays out his theology on life. God is the supreme authority over his life, not you my brothers. God's plans and purposes are greater than any number of events be they good or evil: God is still God. This is a powerful healing therapy if we can embrace God's sovereignty over our life. When you sincerely acknowledge He can turn the worst situation into a redemptive outcome for good, the realisation dawns that nothing can destroy you. This theological truth enables forgiveness to flow more freely. *"And we know that in all things God works for the good of those who love him, who have been called according to his purpose"* (Romans 8:28).

6. HIS WILLINGNESS TO WEEP AND EMBRACE

And he wept so loudly that the Egyptians heard him, and Pharaoh's household heard about it. Then he threw his arms around his brother Benjamin and wept, and Benjamin embraced him, weeping. And he kissed all his brothers and wept over them. Afterwards his brothers talked with him (Genesis 45:2,14-15).

Joseph's choice to forgive and his willingness to express genuine contrition along with the overwhelming joy at re-uniting with his brothers opened the door that broke through their fear and trepidation. This resulted in their genuine expression of joy and reconciliation with Joseph. It took enormous courage but the results were worth the effort. A genuine emotional expression, (as opposed to manipulating crocodile tears), can break down walls of resistance that have existed for years.

7. THEIR RENEWED COMMUNICATION

"Afterwards his brothers talked to him. And he kissed all his brothers and wept over them" (Genesis 45:15). When Joseph restored relationship with his brothers, he immediately restored the bridge of a thirteen year gap in their communication as a family. That is a wonderful benefit of restoration. It is like renewing long–standing friendships you have not seen for a while and the instant feeling of reconnection is awesome.

8. RESTORED A WHOLE FAMILY

Tell my father about all the honour accorded me in Egypt and about everything you have seen. And bring my father down here quickly" (Genesis 45:13).

Joseph never forgot his father's great love for him and he refused to close the door on that significant relationship. That love ultimately brought total healing to their family. In the 21st Century, there is a massive invasion upon our homes and families. Unfortunately there is very little difference between the numbers of divorced Christians to that of non-Christians. In fact "The Barna Group, of Ventura, California, shows that the likelihood of married adults getting divorced is identical among born-again Christians and those who are not born-again." [3]

To bring a balanced perspective to the above quote it should be noted that, "Christianity Today" wrote, "Christians are happier in their marriages and more likely to stay together than non-Christians, new research has found." [4] Terrance Hatch addressing the positives of Christian marriages writes "that the same survey reveals Christian marriages are also the more successful" [5] It appears that the definition of "born–again" in some marriages, could be what creates the conflicting research results. There are genuine born-again Christians and there are nominal Christians who claim to be born again, but fail to live Christ honouring lives. I'm certainly not suggesting genuine born–again Christians do not divorce.

The community at large and the Church specifically need a revival of the Joseph spirit of forgiveness that in spite of the breakdown and lengthy separations, hope for restoration can be renewed in our families. A revival of the urgency to forgive: that means dealing with offences quickly before

> The essence of forgiveness is the choice to relinquish all the resentment, hurt, bitterness, anger, hatred and revenge, exchanging it for freedom.

they have time to fester and destroy our marriages. I consider myself a realist in this area, but I have seen enough of what appeared to be hopeless relationship breakdowns, wonderfully restored through this process of being willing to forgive, exercising humility and making a resolute commitment to restoration. I encourage your prayerful consideration if this is applicable in your life. One such example is the true story of Bill and Ruth (not their real names) who separated, and eventually divorced, neither remarried. Then realising how much they loved each other, committed to remarry again and are enjoying the happiest days of their lives together, according to Bill's own words. I realise this is not everybody's story and some breakdowns appear to be irretrievable, but I am equally sure many breakdowns could be restored with repentance, forgiveness and humility toward each other.

These eight points can serve as a guide for those seeking forgiveness and restoration. There are many professional Christian counsellors willing to walk you through the appropriate restoration process. The multiple benefits received from forgiveness and restoration is worth every pain and stressful moment required to get there.

Here are some of the benefits of forgiveness. The essence of forgiveness is the choice to relinquish all the resentment, hurt, bitterness, anger, hatred and revenge, exchanging it for freedom. It is like opening the birdcage of the soul and setting free that noisy, annoying, irritation of the soul, and exchanging it for the experience of tranquillity of mind and soul as it rests serenely in the awesome sense of peace at last. Then you hear the gentle whisper "it is well with my soul and with my spouse, my neighbour, my work colleague, my Pastor and with my relatives."

1. Nelson Mandela quotes, www.goodreads.com/author/quotes/367338.Nelson_Mandela
2. Dr. Robert Assugioli, www.brainyquote.com/quotes/quotes/r/robertoass311854.html
3. Barna Group, www.barna.com/research/born-again-christians-just-as-likely-to-divorce-as-are-non-christians/#.V7_SA2X26Ls
4. Christianity Today, www.christiantoday.com/article/christian.marriages.have.higher.success.rate/29292.htm
5. Faith Writers, www.faithwriters.com/article-details.php?id=95893

7

A Major Turning Point in Joseph's Life

"But God intended it for Good" (Genesis 50:20).

The life of Joseph is an excellent study of a man whose life experiences exposed him to unwarranted hatred by his brothers, mainly because his fathers' imprudent and overt favouritism toward him. It could be said Joseph was unwise, maybe naïve, even a tad arrogant in the way he shared his dreams with his family, that brought a vitriolic response from his brothers resulting in their plans to dispose of him. He certainty set himself up for further trouble by "snitching" on them. (Genesis 37:2) Be that as it may, Joseph was the recipient of a brutal, disproportionate vendetta from his brothers. Furthermore while diligently serving in Potiphar's house he became the victim of an unjust, falsified sexual charge of attempted rape for which he was sent to jail and was seemingly sentenced to obscurity, overlooked and forgotten.

Although the majority of his early years recorded in the Bible reflected a life of trouble, tragedy and trauma, the latter years were filled with blessing, prosperity and incredible influence as the Prime Minister of Egypt. The life of Joseph is a lesson in God's sovereignty, and His faithfulness toward those who live according to God's word. For Joseph it was a God – birthed dream in his heart that kept him faithful to God's call. From the life of Joseph we can learn that in spite of life's adverse circumstances, if we will steadfastly and resolutely trust God's unfailing love and His promise for

> You know forgiveness is working when you can pray for those who have offended you and you can genuinely pray for them to be blessed

our future, we can be assured He will not fail us.

THE MAJOR TURNING POINT IN JOSEPH'S LIFE – HE ACKNOWLEDGED GOD'S SOVEREIGNTY OVER HIS ENTIRE LIFE

"*...but God sent me ahead of you to preserve for you a remnant on the earth and to save your lives by a great deliverance*" (Genesis 45:7).

Because of his theology of God's sovereignty, Joseph was able to forgive his brothers, which resulted in a threefold blessing in his and their lives.

1. Restoration and emotional healing. That is a heart for reconciliation.
2. Forgiveness without revenge. That is a heart free from past hurts.
3. Forgiveness with blessings for his brothers. That is a heart of magnanimity.

Joseph is a wonderful testimony of a man going beyond "compulsory forgiveness" and displaying a heart of blessing and generosity for those who had once abused him.

Lewis Smedes states, "You will know that forgiveness has begun when you recall those who have hurt you and feel the power to wish them well." [1]

May I suggest for a Christian, you know forgiveness is working when you can pray for those who have offended you and you can genuinely pray for them to be blessed (Romans 12:14)? Forgiveness requires we bless those who persecute us and do not curse them. May I suggest another powerful Biblical principle of dealing with your enemies? Paul instructs us to overcome evil with good. Could I also recommend that you try doing a good deed like buying the person who offended you a coffee, or a small gift? When exercised with a pure motive it can work wonders in both you and them. *"Do not be overcome by evil, but overcome evil with good"*

(Romans 12:21). *"But love your enemies, do good to them, and lend to them without expecting to get anything back. Then your reward will be great, and you will be sons of the Most High, because he is kind to the ungrateful and wicked"* (Luke 6:35). *"If your enemy is hungry, give him food to eat; if he is thirsty, give him water to drink"* (Proverbs 25:21).

When Nelson Mandela became President of South Africa, heads of states from around the globe were invited to his inauguration, no doubt each expecting and vying for front row seats of honour. President Mandela invited his prison guards to sit in those front seats of honour.[2] That is overcoming evil with good.

1. Lewis Smedes, www.brainyquote.com/quotes/quotes/l/lewisbsme132886.html
2. Love Your Enemy, www.higherpraise.com/outlines/woodvale/7_loving6.html

8

The Power of Relinquishing Revenge

In Matthew 18:21-35 Jesus told the parable about a King that was owed a large sum of money by one of his subjects who unfortunately could not repay his debt. So the King demanded he, his wife and children be sold and the money pay for the outstanding debt. The man pleaded with the King for another chance. In Matthew 18: 27 it states the King *"took pity on him and released him from his debt and let him go."*

This same servant that had been released went out and found a fellow servant that owed him a miniscule amount compared to what he had owed the King. But instead of showing mercy to his debtor, he grabbed him around the throat, demanded he be repaid and because the servant could not do so, had him thrown into jail. When the King heard this story, he was so angry; he had the first servant whom the king had previously forgiven, thrown into jail. The main point to be made is that originally the King responded to his servant's plea for mercy, released him and let him go. The word released (apluo) and the words let him go (aphiemi), although similar meanings in the Greek (aphiemi) do have a significant difference and that is "to send forth, to leave, to let go, to send away." The implication is separating from and letting go. I am convinced we may be reluctantly willing to "forgive" someone because Jesus taught us to do so, but we must also "let them go." That means relinquishing all rights and obligations for any revenge, payment, or emotional retribution, and let them walk away free.

> You are not dependant on someone else's response in order for you to exercise forgiveness towards them.

So often the secular response to dealing with offences is reflected in Sigmund Freud's statement, "One must forgive ones enemies, but not before they have been hanged."

For the Christian however the lesson is strong and clear, that our failure to forgive and let go will lead to our personal imprisonment. We can become emotionally captive by what somebody has done to us to the point that we never resolved the issue and they may not even be aware of our offence, nor our captivity. God's pathway to freedom is to forgive and to let go.

FORGIVENESS MAY NOT NECESSARILY INCLUDE RECONCILIATION

The story of Joseph and the reconciliation with his brothers is an ideal goal for all who have been deeply offended in life. However, not all real life conflicts finish up living happily ever after. The reality is, forgiveness is a personal issue. You are not dependant on someone else's response in order for you to exercise forgiveness towards them. Obviously a positive response from them would precipitate a healing process, as in Joseph's case, but their response is not the determining factor. Your choice to forgive is personal and private between you, the offender and God. Remember my personal conflict with my senior pastor; I believed he should have apologised to me. If I had refused to respond to the Holy Spirit's prompting to apologise, I would have been the loser not my pastor.

If your brother sins against you, go and show him his fault, just between the two of you. If he listens to you, you have won your brother over. But if he will not listen, take one or two others along, so that 'every matter may be established by the testimony of two or three witnesses.' If he refuses to listen to them, tell it to the church; and if he refuses to listen even to the church, treat him as you would a pagan or a tax collector. "I tell you the truth, whatever you bind on earth will be bound in heaven, and whatever you loose on earth will be loosed in heaven. "Again, I tell you that if two of you on earth agree about anything you ask for, it will be done for you by my Father in heaven. For where two or three come together in my name, there am I with them." Then Peter came to Jesus and asked, "Lord, how many times shall I forgive my brother when he sins against me? Up to seven times?" Jesus answered, "I tell you, not seven times, but seventy-seven times. "Therefore, the kingdom of heaven is like a king who wanted to settle accounts with his servants. As he began the settlement, a man who owed him ten thousand talents was brought to him. Since he was not able to pay, the master ordered that he and his wife and his children and all that he had be sold to repay the debt. "The servant fell on his knees before him. 'Be patient with me,' he begged, 'and I will pay back everything.' The servant's master took pity on him, cancelled the debt and let him go. "But when that servant went out, he found one of his fellow-servants who owed him a hundred denarii. He grabbed him and began to choke him. 'Pay back what you owe me!' he demanded. "His fellow-servant fell to his knees and begged him, 'Be patient with me, and I will pay you back.' "But he refused. Instead, he went off and had the man thrown into prison until he could pay the debt. When the other servants saw what had happened, they were greatly distressed and went and told their master everything that had happened. "Then the master called the servant in. 'You wicked servant,' he said, 'I cancelled all that debt of yours because you begged me to. Shouldn't you have had mercy on your fellow-servant just as I had on you?' In anger his master turned him over to the jailers to be tortured, until he should pay back all he owed. "This is how my heavenly Father will treat each of you unless you forgive your brother from your heart" (Matthew 18: 15-35).

This passage of scripture identifies the difficulty of attempted reconciliation in the case of a non-respondent brother and the process of endeavouring to bring some closure to the offence committed between two brothers. There may be an argument in this story not to offer forgiveness toward those who refuse to acknowledge their offence. It is obvious there was no repentance nor forgiveness, and certainly no reconciliation in this story. Yet I propose forgiveness is not dependent upon the offender's response because I choose to forgive and let go and in doing so I am set free. Even though we

> For reconciliation to be a reality, both the offender and the offended are required to agree to reconcile.

follow the Biblical procedure and the offender refuses compliance with the church requirements, I can choose to hand him over to God and let him go rather than live in a state of perpetual revenge and un-forgiveness.

One of my ministerial colleagues holds the theological position that forgiveness must be proceeded by, and conditional to repentance. Meaning a person must repent before true forgiveness is offered. His argument is based on God's forgiveness that is freely offered to all humanity, but it only becomes effective in the lives of those who repent and accept Christ, therefore forgiveness is not an automatic blanket of grace, but only to the repentant.

My colleague further believes God offers to all humanity His love and forgiveness. His love is unconditional but forgiveness comes only to those who repent. Although I appreciate my colleagues position, yet when reading this story related to the unrepentant brother, and Peter's question regarding how many times we should offer forgiveness, I am of the opinion in the context of verses 21 and 22 it appears Jesus is teaching unlimited forgiveness and He does not mention the repentance factor of the offender, only forgiveness; nor does He place any conditions on the offender before forgiveness is exercised toward him. Furthermore, Jesus offered a prayer of forgiveness to those who were crucifying him, and they never repented nor sought his forgiveness. *"So Pilate decided to grant their demand"* (Luke 23:24).

However for reconciliation to be a reality, both the offender and the offended are required to agree to reconcile.

Forgiveness can be a personal transaction between you and the offender. If for reasons such as death or you are not able to locate the offender, or there is an unwillingness to be reconciled, we can still exercise personal forgiveness toward them, but not necessarily achieve reconciliation.

9

Forgiveness Sets You Free
From Victimisation

Joseph had every reason to be genuinely offended, and he could have easily fallen into a victim mentality. However, there is no evidence he felt he was poorly done by, nor had God treated him unfairly. It would appear his God–given dream of one day being a leader may have been the positive injection to keep his faith focused and to see that God was still in control in spite of every adverse circumstance. One of the dangers associated with un-forgiveness is that it can lead to self-pity and that can lead to a victim mentality, and unfortunately that can spiral into depression and even suicide.

No doubt, the greater the offense the more difficult it is to forgive.

Forgiving some rude abusive road rage along with all the bad language, finger signs and life threatening comments, would be easier than forgiving American Bernard Madoff for losing my life savings, including my entire retirement fund on his corrupt Ponzi investment scheme, even though he made a public apology as to how sorry he was. However, no matter how disconcerting an apology is in proportion to the devastation caused, it is my choice to forgive him in order that I will be released from his inflicted wound in my heart, although there is no soothing release to my suffering, saddened pocket.

The point I am making is, I understand the ease with which we say the word forgive, and I understand the power released when we do forgive

> Forgiveness is a
> choice of the will
> that is not dependant
> on emotion.

and calculate the consequences attached when refusing to forgive. All that understood it may still make forgiveness a very difficult choice. However it is a better choice than a path of bitterness, hatred and living with a victim mentality for the rest of my life.

Tom Robbins writes – "Don't let yourself be victimised by the age you live in. It's not the times that will bring you down any more than its society. There's a tendency today to absolve individuals of moral responsibility and treat them as victims of social circumstances. You buy that and you pay with your soul. What limits people is lack of character." [1] Victimhood believes "I'm locked into my past. It is not my fault – they did it to me. My parents rejected me, my uncle sexually abused me, my boss unfairly sacked me, my business colleague ripped me off, the Pastor abused my trust, the doctor made a mistake and I am still suffering because of his mistake, the accountant gave me bad advice and cost me dearly. Or the Government did this to me or "THEY" did it to me.

In the movie "Dangerous Minds" actress Michelle Pfeiffer plays the part of an ex-navy seal who is teaching in a rather rough college in the New York Bronx. The previous teacher had lasted only a short time before quitting. Her class consisted of students from disadvantaged homes with the usual challenges of gang warfare, drugs, etc. The major challenge she confronts is their defeatist attitude and the enormous chip of self-pity and victimisation on their shoulders. Boldly addressing the issue on this occasion to her students she makes the following classic statement: "There are no victims in this class room, only choice makers." Although just lines in a movie, I was impressed with the profound truth in that statement. We are all confronted with either a response of being victims or choice makers. Forgiveness is a choice of the will that is not dependant on emotion, but when acted on defeats the victim mentality.

I think Mahatma Gandhi understood not only the reality, but the inevitability of facing offences in life when, he said, "Life is an adventure in forgiveness." I am uncertain exactly what Gandhi had in mind in that statement but I would imagine not too many people would find offences "adventurous." So I suggest in Gandhi's profound wisdom, maybe the adventure is facing and overcoming the offences, maybe it is the satisfaction of victory that Ghandi calls an adventure.

1. Tom Robbins, *Still Life with Woodpecker,* Bantam Doubleday Group Inc. Bantam, U.S.A. 2011, p. 116-117

10

Forgiveness Allows for God's Vengeance

Forgiveness is my willingness to allow God to execute his vengeance as he chooses. The power of forgiveness frees me to hand any negative feelings of revenge or punishment toward my offenders, over to God. *"Vengeance is mine, I will repay, says the Lord"* (Romans 12:19). Forgiveness does not mean we ignore criminal acts such as murder, rape, violence, molestation, robbery, etc. Forgiveness should support the law not neutralise it. I believe it is possible to see justice upheld and still exercise forgiveness toward the offender.

Furthermore, forgiveness does not mean we tolerate repeatable offensive acts of violence by trivialising them. For example, domestic violence must cease. It must never be tolerated under the disguise of exercising forgiveness toward the offender. Nor should we become the defenceless lamb to the slaughter because we incorrectly believe forgiveness means I accept my lot in life and fatalistically capitulate to some bullying, abusing oppressor. Absolutely not! Forgiveness should not be confused with sentiment and false meekness. Handing the vengeance over to God, does not mean covering over criminal acts and acts of violence. Allowing for God's vengeance is not relinquishing justice, but rather maybe it means I will not become the judge, jury and executioner.

No doubt some will disagree with my position and quote Jesus instructing His disciples to take a passive, non-resistant response to those who would demand his bag be carried one mile. *"If someone forces you to go one mile, go with him two miles"* (Matthew 5:41). Jesus in fact required they display an irresistible act of love by going a second mile. However it was Roman authority that a civilian could be required to carry a soldier's bag for one mile.[1]

We see this authority when the Roman soldiers demanded Simon from Cyrene to carry the cross for Christ. *"A certain man from Cyrene, Simon, the father of Alexander and Rufus, was passing by on his way in from the country, and they forced him to carry the cross"* (Mark 15:21). Note it was the law, also it was not cruel bullying, or abusive, although arduous, inconvenient, even unfair and a maybe a violation of modern day human rights. It was not violent abuse of a person, and Jesus was teaching a love response not retaliation to a lawful requirement. That is totally different to violent physical abuse that is unlawful and should not be tolerated. It is possible to forgive, yet not tolerate unlawful violation.

After twenty–seven years in jail on Robben Island, Nelson Mandela had a choice when facing his release. He could either celebrate his freedom by plotting and executing political and radical campaigns of revenge and no doubt a lesser man would seek revenge for the injustice he and his people had received: the right to stand up and fight for justice, racial equality and denounce apartheid were all valid causes. Or he could choose to channel his energies directly to a more positive reform. This was his transforming philosophy: "Don't concentrate on revenge but concentrate on building a better future." On his release he committed to using the law and political process to bring about reform and human rights. Although it is not there yet and is still struggling for equality, his preferred path of reconciliation will eventually prove the better future for his people. Another Mandela quote of great significance regarding forgiveness was, "If there are dreams about a beautiful South Africa, there are also roads that lead to their goal. Two of these roads could be named Goodness and Forgiveness."[2]

Joseph had every right to exercise vengeance, he certainly had the power and authority to exercise punishment over his brothers standing helplessly and confused before him, but he chose forgiveness and left any vengeance issues over to God.

Living in the 21ˢᵗ Century confronts us with numerous overwhelming, unfair and apparent unjust happenings that we believe demand that the punishment should fit the crime, and yet how often we are enraged by the apparent lack of justice. For example the true story of the young policeman who, attempting to break up a brawl, was tackled to the ground smashing his head on the road and received brain injuries that left him unable to continue his previous police duties, yet his attacker walked away free. When interviewed on television the policeman said he intended to get on with his life and not dwell on the past. Another example is that of the young student who was waiting at the bus stop after school at Redcliffe, and the drunk driver being chased by police lost control and kills this lovely innocent girl. When interviewed her mother said, "I am not blaming the police, they had a job to do and blaming them will not bring my daughter back." These are two, true life examples of the apparent lack of justice and yet two examples of people not wishing for punishment on others in order to ease their pain.

Living consumed by vengeance can affect your happiness, your health, and enjoyment for living. Forgive and leave vengeance in God's hands even when the courts may appear to fail. People pursue the legal system with the goal of imposing a just punishment on the offender. If the courts fail to meet that expectation, anger and disappointment are understandable reactions from the victims.

No doubt most of us have witnessed on the television individuals or families leaving the courts frustrated and angry at their perceived failure of the courts to impose an appropriate sentence on the perpetrator of the crime, especially when the crime has brought catastrophe to their family. How long can those families continue to carry the anger relating to their sense of injustice? How do they deal with the bitterness and still live normal healthy emotional lives when carrying a huge sense of injustice and unfairness in their hearts? I can understand that the offended family members would seek a retrial in attempting to correct what they perceived a gross injustice of the law. But having exhausted all avenues of legal justice and failing, where do they go from here? I compassionately recommend a path of forgiveness as a real solution in dealing with such enormous emotional obstacles created by perceived injustice.

> You can't undo anything you've already done, but you can face up to it. You can tell the truth. You can seek forgiveness and then let God do the rest.

Famous T.V. Psychologist and Counsellor, Dr Phil writes: "You have to forgive people, not because they deserve it, but because you deserve to be free of them." [3] Life is too short to be wasted on looking back at the unfair and unjust happenings in our lives.

The Apostle Paul has some excellent advice. *"Brothers, I do not consider myself yet to have taken hold of it. But one thing I do: Forgetting what is behind and straining toward what is ahead, I press on toward the goal to win the prize for which God has called me heavenward in Christ Jesus"* (Philippians 3:13-14).

I read an anonymous quote that has sound advice in dealing with our past and getting on with our future, "You can't undo anything you've already done, but you can face up to it. You can tell the truth. You can seek forgiveness and then let God do the rest."

Are we capable of forgiving anything and everything?

Time magazine had a feature on Forgiveness. They surveyed their readers as to their willingness to forgive certain categories of offences. [4]

	FORGIVE	NOT FORGIVE
Would you forgive someone who has told lies about you?	73%	24%
Stole money from you?	67%	31%
Slapped or punched you in the face?	64%	32%
Held you up with a gun?	42%	54%
Murdered someone in your community?	33%	59%
Raped you?	22%	73%
Raped a member of your family?	19%	77%
Murdered your child?	15%	81%

Do you think you would be capable of offering forgiveness in the following circumstances?

A person who verbally assassinated your character.

A cheating student who replaces your entry into university.

A dishonest broker who lost your life savings.

A spouse who runs off with your best friend.

A person or a gang that bashed your son to death.

A family member or close friend who raped your daughter.

A terrorist who takes the life of a loved one.

A drunk driver who killed your teenage children in a car accident.

The above are just a few real life situations that some people have to live with. How do people cope in such devastating circumstances if there is no forgiveness and emotional closure?

"Time" also ran an article on a lady whose daughter and her boyfriend were brutally murdered. The story majored on this mother's response to the person who committed this heinous crime on her daughter. This is my précis of their story.

Gayle 65, learned to forgive and let go. She said she knew "the big lie" often promised by prosecutors to relatives of murdered victims is that "everything will be OK when the murderer is caught, tried, convicted and executed."

Her nineteen year old daughter and her male friend were stabbed to death on a farm in California. Gayle attended the trial and sentencing of the convicted murderer Douglas Mickey. She heard the date of execution and requested a seat as a witness at his execution. One night before the execution Gayle decided to write to the killer expressing her willingness to forgive him and her desire to visit him in prison. She said "the instant the letter was in the mail box all the anger, all the rage, all the lust for revenge disappeared." Mickey responded to her letter with comments of regret and expressed he was carrying an "unspeakable burden" and wished he could undo that terrible night. Gayle visited Mickey several times and continued to correspond with him. Gayle did not object to the sentence, she did however object to it being done in her name. She said "to murder someone in her name and to say we are doing it for her is horrible." [5] One of the lessons from the Aba Gayle's story is that forgiveness did not translate into a legal pardon.

Forgiveness is not everybody's philosophical persuasion.

Not everybody is sympathetic to the cause of forgiveness. Simon Wiesenthal the Austrian born Jewish survivor of the holocaust became famous as a Nazi hunter after the Second World War. In his book "The Sunflower" he asks the question, should a Jew in a slave camp grant forgiveness to a dying S.S. man begging for absolution? Writer Cynthia Ozick responds with an emphatic absolutely not. She writes "Forgiveness is pitiless, it forgets the victim. It blurs over suffering and death. It drowns the past. The face of forgiveness is mild, but how strong to the slaughtered. Let the S.S. man go to hell." [6] Ozick would not be alone in that particular view. No doubt over the many centuries of World Wars, Racial, Sectarian and Religious wars, there would be millions of return soldiers and civilians all over the world today who would object to hearing forgiveness is the way forward. The painful memories of the atrocities witnessed and experienced, are too much for them to forgive and dismiss.

Although I appreciate those people carrying gruesome, hurtful memories, or even those carrying everyday major offences, the thought of forgiveness is outside their present emotional capacity. I would suggest asking God to allow his grace for forgiveness to flow in your life. Your willingness to make that request could open the door to forgiveness and restoration in your life of the hurtful past.

Phan Thi Kim Phuc is the nine year old girl the world saw running naked down the road after a napalm bomb exploded in her South Vietnamese Village in 1972. Kim is now over forty years of age. She still suffers headaches, poor concentration and other complications from injuries.

She, her husband and young son live in Toronto. Kim is a born–again Christian and says she forgives those soldiers who destroyed her village, killed her relatives and left her permanently scarred. The commander was very sorry, she said.[7]

There can be a supernatural God dimension to forgiveness.

The true story of Corrie Ten Boon is evidence of God's supernatural impartation to forgive, in the life of a woman who survived a Nazi concentration camp. Here is her story.

"It was at a church in Munich that I saw him, the former S.S. man who had stood guard at the shower room door in the processing centre at Ravensbruck. He was the first of our actual jailers that I had seen since that time. And suddenly it was all there – the roomful of mocking, the heaps of clothing, Betsie's pain blanched face.

He came up to me as the church was emptying, beaming and bowing. "How grateful I am for your message Fraulein," he said. "To think that, as you say, 'He has washed my sins away'."

His hand was thrust out to shake mine. And I, who had preached so often to the people in Bloemendaal on the need to forgive, kept my hand at my side.

Even as the angry, vengeful thoughts boiled through me, I saw the sin of them. Jesus Christ had died for this man, was I going to ask for more? Lord Jesus, I prayed, forgive me and help me to forgive him.

I tried to smile; I struggled to raise my hand. I could not. I felt nothing, not the slightest spark of warmth or charity. And so again, I breathed a silent prayer. Jesus, I cannot forgive him. Give him your forgiveness.

As I took his hand, the most incredible thing happened. From my shoulder along my arm and through my hand a current seemed to pass from me to him, while into my heart sprang a love for this stranger that almost overwhelmed me.

And so I discovered that it is not on our forgiveness, any more than on our goodness that the world's healing hinges, but on His. When He tells us to love our enemies, He gives, along with the command, the love itself.[8]

1. *The Pulpit Commentary, Matthew. Volume 15*, Edited H.D.M. Spence and Joseph S. Exell, WM. B. Errdmans Publishing Company, Grand Rapids, Michigan U.S.A. p. 166-167
2. Nelson Mandela, www.brainyquote.com/quotes/quotes/n/nelsonmand178790.html
3. Dr Phil, www.facebook.com/quotes.quotes.quotesxD/posts/452134808157056
4. Time magazine April 5 1999, p. 58
5. ibid.
6. ibid.
7. Colombia Chronicle, The Message of Forgiveness, p. 2
8. Corrie Ten Boom, *The Hiding Place*, Chosen Books, 1971, barrywallace.wordpress.com/2009/03/31/forgiveness-and-corrie-ten-boom/

11

Forgiving Ourselves

"Forgiveness is a gift you give yourself." – Suzanne Summers.

Forgiveness is twofold in terms of not only forgiving others, but we must also forgive ourselves, especially when it comes to accepting God's forgiveness. The enemy of our soul holds incredible power to intimidate by deceiving Christians to underestimate God's grace to forgive and forget. Faith in God's promise to forgive us can be so liberating and emotionally uplifting that we can and should forgive ourselves simply because God has and so should we.

We have no Biblical indication that Joseph regretted or had problems with self-forgiveness. It may be reasonable to assume he regretted telling his dreams to his brothers, or if he regretted snitching on them, but that is pure speculation. His reunion with his brothers had no confession of regret. However I am confident those reading this book like myself have regrets about some aspects of the past, if you could you would have done or said things differently. It is that area of regret or offence that is the breeding ground for not forgiving ourselves.

Forgiving ourselves is based on of God's declaration of His forgiveness for us. When we confess our sins He forgives and forgets our sins and so should we. Do not keep reminding God of what He chooses to forget. *"For I will forgive their wickedness and will remember their sins no more"* (Hebrews 8:12).

Famous American Psychiatrist Karl Menninger (who was awarded the Presidential Medal of Freedom) said, "If he could convince the patients in the psychiatric hospitals that their sins were forgiven, 75% of them could walk out the next day." [1] Although his claim appears to be incredibly high, the point he is making is just how significant self-forgiveness is to our mental, spiritual and emotional well–being. Menninger's quote highlights the corresponding mental and emotional torment experienced when we cannot forgive ourselves.

Intelligent, responsible people are aware of the offences they have caused and the regrettable mistakes they have made. The issue is not only can we forgive others but can we forgive ourselves. I think there are three major issues affecting our ability to forgive ourselves.

1. *The magnitude of the offence or regrettable mistake*

This can range from the huge impact resulting from a car accident that caused death or permanent disability to a person, family, or a number of people. To that of a seemingly insignificant event such as making an innocent humours statement that caused an offence, or unintentionally omitting to acknowledge someone for which they take offence. Clearly the magnitude of offence will determine our ability to forgive ourselves.

2. *The perception of our personal self-worth*

If we have a low self-esteem, offences can be magnified out of proportion. The Bible tells us to love our neighbour as ourselves. If we are battling with a negative self–esteem, life is seen through glasses of self-rejection and we become unduly sensitive to other people and their negative comments. We need to estimate our value in Christ and what He declares about us. This will enable our acceptance of God's estimation of who we are. When we value ourselves from God's perspective and that includes accepting his love and forgiveness toward us. And realising his love is not dependant on our performance talents or abilities, but because of his magnanimous grace. When we truly believe we are born of God and we have his seed of life within us (1 John 3:9). Then this is our true value who we are because of Christ in us the hope of glory (Colossians 1:27). Acknowledging who we are in Christ should deal with false condemnation and raises our true self–esteem that we are accepted by God (Romans 8:1). This realisation can assist us in making faith filled choices to respond in self–forgiveness because of God's abundant forgiveness toward us.

3. Your personality / temperament type

This includes your inclination toward being optimistic which is faith and hope or pessimistic which is fear and doubt. You can choose to operate in optimism (or faith) and believe God can work all things together for good. That choice of faith can open the door to God's abundant grace that can enable you to lift your self-forgiveness by believing that God can change your regrets and offences into victories. God did this for Joseph. The Apostle Paul expresses the essential nature of living according to God's word and not the negativity of our natural mind when he writes *"…be transformed by the renewing of your mind"* (Romans 12:2). That requires engaging your cognitive mental process in line with God's word.

I recommend you seek professional counselling if any of the three areas above are causing you ongoing difficulty.

1. Dr. Karl Menninger, www.sermoncentral.com/illustrations/sermon-illustration-larry-sarver-quotes-forgivenessforothers-forgivenessgeneral-godsforgiveness-2464.asp

fff

12

Forgiveness Can Open the Door to Forgetting and Fruitfulness

"Forgetting what is behind and straining towards what is ahead" (Philippians 3:13).

Genesis 41: 50-52, *"Before the years of famine came, two sons were born to Joseph by Asenath daughter of Potiphera, priest of On. Joseph named his firstborn Manasseh and said, "It is because God has made me forget all my trouble and all my father's household." The second son he named Ephraim and said, "It is because God has made me fruitful in the land of my suffering."*

The Lord had blessed Joseph with two sons. In reflective contemplation, Joseph acknowledges God's goodness and blessing on his life and he calls the firstborn Manasseh, recognising God had enabled him to forget all the troubles in his father's household. He named the second son Ephraim because God had made him fruitful in the land of his suffering.

MANASSEH – GOD HAS MADE ME TO FORGET

When forgetfulness may be a blessing

Time Magazine – May 8th 2008 – their Health section headed up an article entitled "Memory–Forgetting is the new Normal." The article refers to the memory. Researcher Dr. Scott Small who assures us memory loss does not mean you are losing your wits. He provides a rather technical explanation of why our memory fails us on occasions and he calms down the over anxiety that we are all heading for Alzheimer's. He does however point

> When we acknowledge and confess our sins God chooses to forgive and forget our past.

out that Alzheimer's is expected to affect 34 million people globally by the year 2025.

The point I am endeavouring to make is unless old age or poor memory is our lot in life, most of us will find it very difficult to forget hurtful memories. For those who have lost a loved one in tragic or regrettable circumstances, I understand forgetting may be beyond their natural capability to even attempt. Certainly in the early days of grieving it is probably impossible for the majority of people to even contemplate this forgetting issue. I do question the well–meaning, but often the glib advise of those who say " Time heals" or "you will get over it " because that is not necessary true. For some who have experience deep grief and unbearable sense of loss, their best hope is learning to live with the loss. I certainly reject the notion I heard one speaker say that grief is like a fly on your arm that needs brushing away. I am not sure which world he lives in but it is different to mine, and for the vast majority of people I have witnessed facing grief and offences, they would not relate to his statement either. In fact they would probably be angry at such a frivolous proposition.

Hopefully I have conveyed my understanding and appreciation for those who experience the reality and severity of offences people carry in their life. However, I suggest there are two aspects to this Biblical forgetting that Joseph experienced that may apply in our lives.

1. THE FORGETTING FACTOR – GOD CHOOSES TO FORGET

When we acknowledge and confess our sins God chooses to forgive and forget our past. *"Their sins and lawless deeds I will remember no more"* (Hebrews 10:17). *"For I will be merciful to their unrighteousness, and their sins and their lawless deeds I will remember no more"* (Hebrews 8:12. NKJV).

This Omniscient, Transcendent, Supremely Intelligent, Holy God – chooses to forget. WOW! When we rehearse those hurtful events and offences and seek revenge on the perpetrators in our thought life, we reignite the pain all over again. The offence may have occurred only once but we have the choice to revisit and replay that event repeatedly, to our detriment. It could possibly be motivated by some morbid, self–indulgence which we know is deleterious to our emotional, physical and spiritual well-being. Yet in our replaying the past, we remind God of what He chose to forgive and forget.

Therefore our first responsibility is self-discipline; we make the choice of refusing to constantly dwell on the past. Retrospective thinking will paralyse your progress in life, hinder your Spiritual development, and dampen your faith, especially when we constantly dwell on our past offenses or our specific failures.

Lot's wife is a prime example of the danger in disobediently looking back to Sodom when God had clearly and specifically told her not to do so, and she became a pillar of salt, paralysed in her pursuit to escape Sodom. *But Lot's wife looked back, and she became a pillar of salt* (Genesis 19:26).

Paul warns against retrospective vision, he writes in Philippians 3:13, *"Brothers and sisters, I do not consider myself yet to have taken hold of it. But one thing I do: Forgetting what is behind and straining toward what is ahead."*

Forgetting – Paul uses the Greek word 'epilanthanomai' which means to lose out of the mind, by implication to neglect thinking about the past. This is the opposite of constantly remembering the past. It is unhealthy to constantly reflect on past problems, failures, hurts and offences. Paul may have been making reference to the previous verses on his Jewish legalistic past. He may have in mind that he was a blasphemer, a violent man. *"Even though I was once a blasphemer and a persecutor and a violent man, I was shown mercy because I acted in ignorance and unbelief"* (1Timothy 1:13), or maybe referring to his regrets as a persecutor of the early Church, or his rigid Pharisaic intolerance. But one thing is clear, forgetting the past allows us to strain toward God's future for us. One of the areas of conflict in a marriage is a spouse who constantly brings up past mistakes or failures. It is so destructive and needs to be dealt with, either by applying a 1 Corinthians 13:5 style of love that "keeps no record of wrong" or by exercising a forgiveness that chooses to forget the offences. Having made the point of choosing to forgive and forget it is of equal importance the offended person does not experience repeatable offences; in particular in such areas as infidelity, incest and physical violence. When forgiveness is sought and given it is essential there is evidence of genuine repentance for the offence. John the Baptist calls this the *"fruits of repentance"* (Matthew 3:8). Paul reinforces this point when he explains his conversion and his God–given ministry mandate to King Agrippa, ensuring his preaching included repentance involved turning away from sin. *"I preached that they should repent and turn to God and prove their repentance by their deeds"* (Acts 26:20). The point to be emphasised is the unfair burden that is imposed on a person genuinely offering forgiveness and genuinely desiring forgetfulness when there are repeated offences. It should be also noted "fruit of repentance" requires time to grow, and that may be months and years not just days or weeks.

THE POWER OF REFOCUS

The writer of Hebrews acknowledges that in order to effectively run this Christian race of life we need to deal with the weights (and sins) that impede our progress. The word weight (onkos) refers to mass, impediment, body: it refers in a negative sense to inner spiritual weight which accrues to something. Although not specifically referring to forgetting our past, I think it could include such "weightiness." *"Therefore, since we are surrounded by such a great cloud of witnesses, let us throw off everything that hinders and the sin that so easily entangles, and let us run with perseverance the race marked out for us. Let us fix our eyes on Jesus, the author and perfecter of our faith, who for the joy set before him endured the cross, scorning its shame, and sat down at the right hand of the throne of God Consider him who endured such opposition from sinful men, so that you will not grow weary and lose heart. In your struggle against sin, you have not yet resisted to the point of shedding your blood. And you have forgotten that word of encouragement that addresses you as sons: "My son, do not make light of the Lord's discipline, and do not lose heart when he rebukes you, because the Lord disciplines those he loves, and he punishes everyone he accepts as a son." Endure hardship as discipline; God is treating you as sons. For what son is not disciplined by his father? If you are not disciplined (and everyone undergoes discipline), then you are illegitimate children and not true sons. Moreover, we have all had human fathers who disciplined us and we respected them for it. How much more should we submit to the Father of our spirits and live! Our fathers disciplined us for a little while as they thought best; but God disciplines us for our good, that we may share in his holiness. No discipline seems pleasant at the time, but painful. Later on, however, it produces a harvest of righteousness and peace for those who have been trained by it"* (Hebrews 12: 1-11).

The writer of Hebrews also strongly recommends "looking unto Jesus" who is our perfect example. He who has tasted the offences of life triumphed through them. The example of Jesus highlights seeing the big picture, He saw himself sitting at the right hand of the Father. Focusing on the eternal is not escapism, nor is it refusing to face the realities of here and now. Focusing on Jesus and the eternal issues assists in bringing some of the cruel issues of life into an eternal perspective. Joseph had a long–term perspective to his life and the promise God had planted in his heart when he was but a youth.

A FAITH FOCUS NOT A FATALISTIC FOCUS

One of the great heroes of faith is Job. He had every imaginable hurt, offence, trail and negative circumstance humanly possible. Yet he triumphed in faith. This Godly man suffered loss of family, cattle, servants, homes and health. Every area of his life was affected, emotionally, financially, physically and socially. For example, his wife and friends were negative, his wife told him to curse God and die. *His wife said to him, "Are you still holding on to your integrity? Curse God and die!"* (Job 2:9). So impeccable was Job's integrity and his unwavering faith in the Almighty that he makes the ultimate confession of trust in God. *"Though he slay me yet will I trust him"* (Job 13:15). The scripture records the latter days of Job's life were so blessed of the Lord that He gave him twice as much as he had in the beginning, and he saw his fourth generation of grandchildren: he lived to be one hundred and forty years old. Job was a man with a "faith focus" in the midst of overwhelming adverse circumstances.

We should never forget what Christ has achieved in our lives. The love of God, the Cross, His Resurrection life, the outpouring of the Holy Spirit are good and healthy memories. I am sure these are some of the "whatsoever things are lovely and of a good report" that are good to dwell on, as opposed to dwelling on our past hurts and offences.

2. THE SUPERNATURAL FACTOR IN FORGETTING

The second aspect to forgetting in the context of the story of Joseph is the supernatural ability of God that enables us to forget. Only God can perform that supernatural amnesia. Manasseh represents a new grace gift of God in Joseph's life: this new focus – this new life – this new possibility and the fulfilment of his God-given dream. This became the new focus in Joseph's life. Over the years in ministry I have witnessed many emphasises on "Healing of the Memories" and bringing up the past negative experiences and dealing with them. I am sure there is a benefit in some people's lives to deal with specific areas of torment relating to the past in order for them to progress into the future. But I do believe in the application of Christ's blood to cleanse me from all my sins. *"How much more, then, will the blood of Christ, who through the eternal Spirit offered himself unblemished to God, cleanse our consciences from acts that lead to death, so that we may serve the living God!"* (Hebrews 9:14). This is a starting point to break the power from all my past sin, hurts and offences. We read in 1 John1:9, *"If we confess our sins, he is faithful and just and will forgive us our sins and purify us from all unrighteousness."* The confession of our sins provides God's forgiveness and cleansing.

The Manasseh principle is a powerful gift of God's grace that enables you to take a forward step into God's plan for your life.

The Scripture promises us a *"crown of beauty for ashes, the oil of joy for mourning, and a garment of praise for a spirit of despair"* (Isaiah 61:3). These are just some of God's "replacement" promises for the disappointments and offences in life. The Manasseh principle is a powerful gift of God's grace that enables you to take a forward step into God's plan for your life.

Manasseh (forgetting) helps live beyond false guilt and false punishment.

When Joseph's brothers are standing before him, not knowing who he was, they are smitten with guilt and shame, listen to their words from Genesis 42: 21 *"They said to one another, "surely we are being punished because of our brother. We saw how distressed he was when he pleaded with us for his life, but we would not listen; that's why this distress is come upon us."*

Living in unresolved past hurts, whether victim or perpetrator, those memories may create a sense of anticipated punishment when things go wrong. This is a cruel torment of mind to believe the guilt's of the past are catching up with me now in my present difficulty. This was the same reaction the widow of Zarephath had to the death of her son. She accused Elijah of bringing judgement on her son because of her past sins.

> When we seek God's forgiveness we need to live a faith filled life, rather than having a tormented frame of mind of expecting our past to punish us.

Sometime later the son of the woman who owned the house became ill. He grew worse and worse, and finally stopped breathing, She said to Elijah, "What do you have against me, man of God? Did you come to remind me of my sin and kill my son?" "Give me your son," Elijah replied. He took him from her arms, carried him to the upper room where he was staying, and laid him on his bed. Then he cried out to the LORD, "O LORD my God, have you brought tragedy also upon this widow I am staying with, by causing her son to die?" Then he stretched himself out on the boy three times and cried to the LORD, "O LORD my God, let this boy's life return to him!" The LORD heard Elijah's cry, and the boy's life returned to him, and he lived. Elijah picked up the child and carried him down from the room into the house. He gave him to his mother and said, "Look, your son is alive!" Then the woman said to Elijah, "Now I know that you are a man of God and that the word of the LORD from your mouth is the truth" (1 Kings 17:17-24).

The great news of the Gospel is we can know our past is forgiven and forgotten—one of the major benefits of the New Covenant. Hebrews 8:12 says, *"I will forgive their wickedness and will remember their sins no more."* GOD CHOOSES TO FORGET OUR SINS and we must choose to accept that forgiveness and stop living under the guilt of expected punishment for that which is our cleansed past, living rather in the faith that my past is forgiven and forgotten from God's perspective. This can enable me to live free of expecting punishment from my past and live with an expectation of blessing for the future.

However, living in forgiveness and forgetfulness would not be balanced without pointing out that there can be consequences to our past. For example an unmarried pregnant lady coming to Christ and confessing the sins of her past life does not remove the unborn child. David and Bathsheba, in spite of David's repentance prayer, still carried the consequence of their sin.

The point I am making here is this. When we seek God's forgiveness we need to live a faith filled life, rather than having a tormented frame of mind of expecting our past to punish us. However we must equally acknowledge there may be an obvious consequence to our past.

fff

13

Living Beyond Perceived Unfairness

"Your pain is the breaking of the shell that encloses your understanding."
Kahil Gidran.

It is difficult to read the life of Joseph without concluding he had more than his share of life's unfairness. His brothers' hating him because he was Dad's favourite; thrown into jail for refusing the sexual advances of Potiphar's wife and her trumped up charge of attempted rape and sitting in jail, seemingly forgotten. These would be major areas of perceived unfairness for most of us if we were Joseph.

Job exhibited living beyond perceived unfairness.

The story of Job would also appear incredibly unfair to any casual observer who failed to see the sovereignty of the God factor in his life. He was a righteous man, a good family man, an astute businessman, very wealthy, happy and healthy. Everything was going great when suddenly everything goes unbelievably wrong. He lost his children, his homes, his cattle, his

> The only conclusion I have come to is we perceive life to be unfair because we fail to see God's hidden purpose for our lives.

servants, and his health. Surely these are massive areas of unfairness in the life of a godly man.

The only conclusion I have come to is we perceive life to be unfair because we fail to see God's hidden purpose for our lives. That is why Christianity is called a walk of faith. We believe God is the supreme authority and worthy of our trust. Even though we may not know why unfair things happen, we believe Romans 8:28, *"all things work together for good to those who love God to those who are called according to His purpose."* The response of Job in what must have been confusing circumstances as recorded in Job 1:22, *"In all this, Job did not sin by charging God with wrong doing."* That is an incredible faith level in what appears to be unfair and extreme circumstances of life. I therefore conclude, that all God's ways must be right for his character is righteous and his ways are perfect. *"The LORD is righteous in all his ways and loving towards all he has made"* (Psalm 145:17).

THERE ARE GOD BLAMERS

There are many people who unlike Job blame God for the offences, hurts, and tragedies of life. When the children of Israel were delivered from Egypt and crossed the Red sea witnessing the defeat of the Egyptians, they rejoiced with singing and dancing. When things went wrong they blamed God, Moses everything and everybody except themselves and their lack of faith.

Reflecting on the life of Joseph and his ability to forgive his brothers, and reflecting on the teaching and example of Christ in regards to forgiveness, and His teaching to love our enemies, to pray for those who hate you, I am convinced forgiveness may appear to be unreasonable, unnatural, unfair, undeserved. But undoubtedly it is God's solution to the untold offences of life and one of those keys to living in joy and happiness – that is the Kingdom of God. So forgiveness may appear unfair but clearly God does know best and all his ways are perfect. Philip Yancy writes "The only thing harder than forgiveness is the alternative." [1]

---

1. Philip Yancy, *What's So Amazing About Grace?*, Zondervan, Grand Rapids, Michigan 1997

14

Forget the Trouble in my Father's Household

Genesis 41:51 – *"God has made me forget all my trouble and my father's household."*

TROUBLES IN THE NATURAL HOUSEHOLD

Joseph had a dysfunctional family that is clearly evidenced by the hatred, bitterness and rejection from his brothers. All his troubles started in his household. Psychologist Dr. Charles Solomon believes "Rejection is one of the prime causes of psychological disturbances." [1] "Parental rejection has to be one of the most damaging." Dr. Solomon warns parents of the damage caused by what he calls "Covert and Overt rejection" of their children.

Overt rejection means obvious comments of rejection such as "we wish you had never been born" or "we wanted a daughter, not you" or "you have disrupted this family." Children being given out for adoption or to an orphanage would be an obvious evidence of parental rejection. Realising there could have been genuine reasons for adoption beyond the control of the mother, as was the case in this country many years ago, when the removal of a new born child was given out for adoption without the mother's permission and in most cases without her even seeing her new born baby.

Covert rejection Dr. Solomon suggests, is where the parents indulge in extreme pampering and protection of the child to the point of providing

> Rejection will affect every area of your life and stifle your fruitfulness.

no boundaries or guidelines for the child's development and maturity, which Solomon suggests breeds insecurity and rejection.[2] Joseph acknowledged his family troubles, the rejection, the bitterness and hatred yet God enabled him to forget those troubled years and rise to incredible influence and authority.

The story of Ahithophel: A man who could not handle rejection.

Absalom said to Ahithophel, "Give us your advice. What should we do?" Ahithophel answered, "Lie with your father's concubines whom he left to take care of the palace. Then all Israel will hear that you have made yourself an offence to your father's nostrils, and the hands of everyone with you will be strengthened." So they pitched a tent for Absalom on the roof, and he lay with his father's concubines in the sight of all Israel. Now in those days the advice Ahithophel gave was like that of one who enquires of God. That was how both David and Absalom regarded all of Ahithophel's advice" (2 Samuel 16:20-23). *"When Ahithophel saw that his advice had not been followed, he saddled his donkey and set out for his house in his home town. He put his house in order and then hanged himself. So he died and was buried in his father's tomb"* (17:23).

The advice of Ahithophel was like the word of the Lord to David and Absalom (vs. 23) except on this one occasion. Sadly he could not handle the rejection, he rode home put his house in order and hanged himself: what a tragic end to a brilliant godly adviser. There are many Pastors, ex-board members and once effective leaders sitting around Churches that are angry, negative and troublesome because their advice was not listened to by the leadership. Should that identify your situation please exercise forgiveness, for your benefit, your family's benefit and the church you attend. Rejection will affect every area of your life and stifle your fruitfulness.

Joseph was the recipient of rejection, hatred and abuse by his brothers. This rejection and overt hatred ultimately manifested itself by selling him to some Midianite traders on their way to Egypt. Maybe you were a recipient of rejection, physical, emotional or sexual abuse in your household. You may need to seek professional counselling, for you will no doubt understand, time does not automatically heal the pain and hurt of those past traumas.

May I respectfully recommend praying that God will heal the trouble of your father's household? May He grant you the birth of a Spiritual Manasseh; one that reveals God's Father heart of love and acceptance toward you.

SPIRITUAL HOUSEHOLD

Many christians become offended inside the church household.

There are a multitude of reasons why people leave the church. In this book we are dealing in particular with those who leave because they are offended.

Referring again to David Huskey and his research that indicates 66% of people leave the church because they are offended. Surely of the 34% that remain in the church, it would not necessarily indicate they have not been offended but rather it could indicate a percentage of them may be sitting in the church with unresolved offences, or they have resolved the offence and chosen to move on with their life and remain in the church. Whatever the reasons for the 66% of offended people leaving, it is an alarming percentage of offended people that would have a detrimental effect on the average congregation. I pray they resolve that offence by forgiveness before attending the next church. This highlights one of the reason's we are addressing the subject of forgive, forget, fruitfulness.

Tragically the church has failed the Lord and the Community.

The sexual abuse of children by the clergy and church leaders is intolerable and appalling. Although my subject 'forgive, forget, fruitful' may appear a little trite to victims of sexual and other abuses, I can understand the demand for a Royal Commission, that may not only provide the opportunity for people to be heard, but hopefully procedures will be put in place to minimise further abuses. However I do believe that with God's help along with professional counselling, love and care, there is a path to freedom and restoration. There are a few Pastors and Church leadership who have been abused by congregations. These are mainly verbal and emotional abuses but they can devastate the whole family. G. Lloyd Rediger, Author, conference speaker and consultant, wrote a book entitled "Clergy Killers" addressing who these people are that attack the clergy and how this phenomenon is growing. I have seen many Senior Pastors crying because of the abuse and rejection by members in their congregation. Should there be a Pastor or Church leader reading this book that identifies with receiving such abuse, could I encourage you to choose to forgive, ask God for a Manasseh to be birthed in your heart that will enable you to forget all the troubles in the Church household. If needed, seek Godly professional help. I have seen God's grace heal and restore Pastors and people back to normality and fruitfulness.

1. Dr Charles R. Solomon, *The Ins and Out of Rejection*, Heritage House Publications, Denver, Colorado U.S.A. 1976 p. 30
2. ibid. p. 40-47

fff

15

The Similarity Between Joseph and Jesus

Aligning the troubles of Joseph with the troubles of Jesus is a healthy exercise in order to understand and identify with the human side of Christ's life, suffering and His capacity to heal and restore lives today.

JOSEPH was troubled by his brethren. Joseph was hated, despised, rejected and eventually sold by his brothers to some travelling merchants.

JESUS was troubled by His brethren. *"He came to that which was His own, but his own did not receive him"* (John 1: 11). The religious leaders eventually had Him crucified. The Prophet Isaiah described prophetically what Jesus would suffer on this planet. *"He was despised and forsaken of men, a man of sorrows and acquainted with grief"* (Isaiah 53:3). Jesus understands rejection and abuse and can minister from his compassion.

JOSEPH was tempted. Potiphars wife endeavoured to seduce him, *"and after a while his master's wife took notice of Joseph and said, 'Come to bed with me!'"* (Genesis 39:7). Joseph is a prime example of how a person with a sense of destiny can triumph in life's temptations.

JESUS was tempted in all ways as we are, yet without sin. *"For we do not have a high priest who is unable to sympathise with our weaknesses, but we have one who has been tempted in every way, just as we are—yet was without sin"* (Hebrews 4:15). The most obvious temptation was after the 40 days in prayer and fasting when Satan personally came and tempted Him. Here we see a great lesson on dealing with temptation, for Jesus triumphed by quoting *"It is written"* (Matthew 4:1-11). Christ's great defence against Satan's deception was the word of God. That same defence is ours; using the word of God applies in our lives.

JOSEPH was troubled by hardship. Working for Potiphar and then working in the prison. This was not a life of ease and opulence, but the hardship was a part of his training to become the National Leader. Learning to serve is always a sure path to leadership development.

JESUS was troubled by hardship. He was born in a stable, worked as a carpenter, no silver spoon in His life. He understands the struggles of life. *"He came not to be served but to serve and give His life a ransom for many"* (Matthew 20:28).

JOSEPH was troubled by isolation. A Hebrew in Egypt separated from his family and friends, living in a different culture; a pagan religion and National events were totally different. He had some major re-adjustments to make in this land of Egypt.

JESUS was troubled by isolation. This is more than an International culture challenge. This is God on earth. This is the Holy God, the Creator of the world, choosing to identify with His creation. He became flesh, living, eating, sleeping and building friendships among humanity. Jesus the Son of God was also Jesus the son of man: fully God, fully man.

> In Christ we have been granted the grace for the forgiveness of sin, and His grace to assist us in forgetting our past.

The reason I have taken the time to address some of the similarities between Joseph and Jesus is in order to assist us in identifying with the humanity of Christ and to realize He was subject to the same emotions and rejections, heartaches and disappointments that we go through. In doing so, we know that He is touched with the feelings of our infirmities. *"For we do not have a high priest who is unable to sympathize with our weaknesses, but we have one who has been tempted in every way, just as we are —yet he did not sin"* (Hebrews 4:15).

In Christ we have been granted the grace for the forgiveness of sin, and His grace to assist us in forgetting our past. As Christians, we have the great privilege of extending God's grace in forgiving and forgetting those who have offended us, clearing a path of openness and transparency with God and other people. I encourage your diligent application to this area of forgiving and forgetting. If there is a tormenting memory in the past, ask the Lord to grant you a gracing of the Holy Spirit to birth a spiritual 'Manasseh' in your life (Genesis 41:51). The birth of Manasseh reminded Joseph that God had enabled him to forget all his troubles and in particular relating to his household. I've encouraged the need and willingness to forgive, but I realise for some the magnitude of the hurt never seems to go away. This is when we need a supernatural enabling of the Holy Spirit to forget all those past hurts. This enables us to forget the pain and live a happy healthy live.

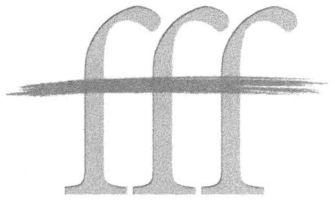

16

God's Grace for an Ephraim

Joseph declared the reason he had named his second son Ephraim was that, *"God has made me fruitful in the land of my suffering"* (Genesis 41:52). The Hebrew word for 'fruitful' is "Parah"… meaning to cause to be fruitful, to grow, to increase.

The Pulpit Commentary renders it as "double fruitfulness" or "double land." Clearly the name Ephraim suggests to us that the adverse circumstances of life are many times the instruments through which God brings our adjustment and maturity. He does this in order to mould us into Christ's image and to bring God's fruitfulness or double blessings on our lives. This is a repetitive theme in scripture

In this you greatly rejoice, though now for a little while you may have had to suffer grief in all kinds of trials. These have come so that your faith—of greater worth than gold, which perishes even though refined by fire—may be proved genuine and may result in praise, glory and honour when Jesus Christ is revealed. Though you have not seen him, you love him; and even though you do not see him now, you believe in him and are filled with an inexpressible and glorious joy (1 Peter 1:6-8).

Tough times refine our faith to prove how genuine it is and brings glory to God.

James, a servant of God and of the Lord Jesus Christ, To the twelve tribes scattered among the nations: Greetings. Consider it pure joy, my brothers, whenever you face trials of many kinds, because you know that the testing of

your faith develops perseverance. Perseverance must finish its work so that you may be mature and complete, not lacking anything (James 1:1-4).

Trials develop perseverance that in turn brings maturity and completeness. We must therefore live in faith and forgiveness, for many of the offences and grievous events caused by others are God's path to our maturity. This principle is abundantly evident in the life of Joseph. Mark Twain is credited with saying "Forgiveness is the fragrance that the flower leaves on the heel of the one who crushed it." How true for a Christian, that some of the pains in life bring out the fragrance of Christ's life in us.

The Ephraim factor in our lives enables us to face the hurts, disappointments, heartaches, tragedies and sometimes those huge unfairnesses and still have the sense of God achieving his purpose in our maturity through it all. The Ephraim factor energises my faith in a loving Heavenly Father who knows what is best for me, knowing that His Master plan is best for my long-term development and in particular the eternal purposes he has in mind. Surely this is what the Scripture is enforcing in 2 Corinthians 4:17-18, *"For our light and momentary troubles are achieving for us an eternal glory that far outweighs them all. So we fix our eyes not on what is seen, but on what is unseen. For what is seen is temporary, but what is unseen is eternal."*

Again Paul puts a strong emphasis on the eternal rewards of our life when he writes… *"I consider that our present sufferings are not worth comparing with the glory that will be revealed in us"* (Rom. 8:18). He further stresses we must take care on how we build and what materials we use for they will be tested by fire (1 Corinthians 3: 10-15). Peter reinforces this eternal perspective when he writes… *"And we look to that day when the Chief shepherd shall appear and we will receive a crown of Glory that will never fade away"* (1 Peter 5:4).

> One of the negative effects of secularism in our modern society has been its ability to rob us of the eternal perspective of life.

One of the negative effects of secularism in our modern society has been its ability to rob us of the eternal perspective of life. We are eternal beings with an eternal destiny. This life is preparation for that eternal destination.

The Ephraim factor prevents us from running or quitting when things get tough. There is a sociological phenomenon that contributes to the high transient population in most Western Nations. Simply put, when things get tough such as conflicts with my neighbour or with the boss at work, or the kids do not like school, people simply up and leave. The Americans call it the "rootlessness syndrome." The highest transient cities in America are Las Vegas and Washington, D.C. Both have a 30.68% annual turnover. New York has a 28.41% turnover per annun. These are the three highest transient cities in the U.S.A.[1] This is a real social problem in terms of stability and business momentum. Unfortunately it affects many of our church congregations in terms of stability, reliability and affecting the process of maturing the saints. They simply don't sit still long enough for maturity and ministry development to take place. Prayerful consideration should be given to those who have occupations that require compulsory frequent relocations, such as the military, schoolteachers and government employees etc.

Rootless Christians will not grow and mature, they are pot bound, usually constrained by the limitations of ideal circumstances. Unfortunately most churches do not exist in the ideal world, but the real world. The Psalmist writes… *"He is like a tree planted by streams of water, which yields its fruit in season and whose leaf does not wither. Whatever he does prospers"* (Psalm 1:3). This encourages us that in order to be fruitful, we need to be like a tree PLANTED. Good roots bring forth good fruits. Put your roots down in a good Bible believing church that loves Jesus with all their hearts and has a passion for the lost and quit drifting.

The Ephraim Factor brings God's divine blessing and increase. The story of Joseph is a story of God's faithfulness and His reward towards those who are faithful to Him.

This is clearly evident in Joseph's progression from a prison to Prime Minister.

However, we should not calculate blessing and prosperity as being restricted to financial or material measurements only. Surely health, happiness, family, friendships and fulfilling a sense of God's purpose in our life are major considerations in defining blessing and prosperity.

Joseph reflects his high value on family when he insists his father and family join him in Egypt as an urgent and top priority. He refused to allow the wealth, influence and prestige of his Prime Ministerial position blind him of the true basic values of life. The fact that he acknowledged he was living in God's purpose for his life, I suggest, was a major contributing factor in his declaration that "God had made him fruitful in the land of his suffering." When we honour God in our life decisions, He will surely honour us. *"Humility and the fear of the LORD bring wealth and honour and life"* (Proverbs 22: 4).

The Ephraim factor of fruitfulness is obviously manifest in Joseph's high profile position and great influence as Prime Minister. We all have the God given opportunity to influence others for good and for the Gospel. We may never become a Prime Minister or President but we can exert Godly influence. I encourage you to expect an Ephraim grace upon your life of increased influence for the Kingdom of God.

EPHRAIM RECEIVES THE RIGHT HAND OF BLESSING

Jacob said to Joseph, "God Almighty appeared to me at Luz in the land of Canaan, and there he blessed me4 and said to me, 'I am going to make you fruitful and will increase your numbers. I will make you a community of peoples, and I will give this land as an everlasting possession to your descendants after you.' "Now then, your two sons born to you in Egypt before I came to you here will be reckoned as mine; Ephraim and Manasseh will be mine, just as Reuben and Simeon are mine. Any children born to you after them will be yours; in the territory they inherit they will be reckoned under the names of their brothers. As I was returning from Paddan, to my sorrow Rachel died in the land of Canaan while we were still on the way, a little distance from Ephrath. So I buried her there beside the road to Ephrath" (that is, Bethlehem). When Israel saw the sons of Joseph, he asked, "Who are these?" "They are the sons God has given me here," Joseph said to his father. Then Israel said, "Bring them to me so that I may bless them." Now Israel's eyes were failing because of old age, and he could hardly see. So Joseph brought his sons close to him, and his father kissed them and embraced them. Israel said to Joseph, "I never expected to see your face again, and now God has allowed me to see your children too." Then Joseph removed them from Israel's knees and bowed down with his face to the ground. And Joseph took both of them, Ephraim on his right towards Israel's left hand and Manasseh on his left towards Israel's right hand, and brought them close to him. But Israel reached out his right hand and put it on Ephraim's head, though he was the younger, and crossing his arms, he put his left hand on Manasseh's head, even though Manasseh was the firstborn. Then he blessed Joseph and said, "May the God before whom my fathers Abraham and Isaac walked, the God who has been my shepherd all my life to this day, the Angel who has delivered me from all harm—may he bless these boys. May they be called by my name and the names of my fathers Abraham and Isaac, and may they increase greatly upon the earth." When Joseph saw his father placing his right hand on Ephraim's head he was displeased; so he took hold of his father's hand to move it from Ephraim's head to Manasseh's head. Joseph said to him, "No, my father, this one is the firstborn; put your right hand on his head." But his father refused and said, "I know, my son, I know. He too will become a people, and he too will become great. Nevertheless, his younger brother will be greater than he, and his descendants will become a group of nations." He blessed them that day and said, "In your name will Israel pronounce this blessing: 'May God make you like Ephraim and Manasseh.'" So he put Ephraim ahead of Manasseh (Genesis 48:3-20).

Joseph brought his two sons before his father ISRAEL for him to impart his Patriarchal blessing. We should never underestimate the SIGNIFICANCE of TRANSFERRED BLESSING and POWER BY LAYING ON OF HANDS. This is also a New Testament principle of impartation of life, power, authority, setting aside for ministry, healing the sick, receiving the Baptism in the Holy Spirit and many other practical applications of impartations. The laying on of hands is a God idea of impartation and we should take the opportunities as they arise to allow God to use us as a conduit of His power and blessing.

Joseph was committed to 'transferred impartation' from a Godly Patriarch. A word of caution, take great care in selecting who you allow to impart into your life, check their life not just their gift.

THE RIGHT HAND ON THE YOUNGEST SON

When Joseph saw his father placing his right hand on Ephraim's head he was displeased; so he took hold of his father's hand to move it from Ephraim's head to Manasseh's head. Joseph said to him, "No, my father, this one is the firstborn; put your right hand on his head." But his father refused and said, "I know, my son, I know. He too will become a people, and he too will become great. Nevertheless, his younger brother will be greater than he, and his descendants will become a group of nations" (Genesis 48:17-19).

Joseph rightly thought he was correcting a simple mistake by his father who had placed his right hand on Ephraim, the younger son instead of Manasseh. However, his father was quick to let Joseph know there was no mistake and Ephraim was God's chosen leader over his older brother. The right hand signified the first and rightful blessing to the eldest son. But here again, without explanation, God sovereignly chose and revealed through the prophetic authority on Israel, that the younger brother would be over the elder. This is not the only occasion for this reversed blessing. God did this with many others such as Abel over Cain, with Shem over Japheth, with Isaac over Ishmael, and many others including the classic of David being chosen over his seven older brothers.

So Samuel took the horn of oil and anointed him in the presence of his brothers, and from that day on the Spirit of the LORD came upon David in power. Samuel then went to Ramah (1 Samuel 16:13).

Our main character Joseph was the youngest of his brothers at the time of these conflicts; we do know the biblical record indicates Benjamin was born after Joseph.

Not only that, but Rebekah's children had one and the same father, our father Isaac. Yet, before the twins were born or had done anything good or bad—in order that God's purpose in election might stand: not by works but by him who calls—she was told, "The older will serve the younger." Just as it is written:

"Jacob I loved, but Esau I hated." What then shall we say? Is God unjust? Not at all! For he says to Moses, "I will have mercy on whom I have mercy, and I will have compassion on whom I have compassion." It does not, therefore, depend on man's desire or effort, but on God's mercy (Romans 9: 10-16).

The scripture clearly indicates God chooses whomever He sovereignly wills, according to His purpose and pleasure and without any obvious external influence such as physical appearance, intelligence or popularity. This scripture reinforces that point by stating that God chose Jacob over Esau while they were still in their mother's womb.

1. *What are the most transient cities in the United States?* – City-Data Forum, www.city-data.com/forum/city-vs-city/586188-what-most-transient-cities-united-states-3.html

17

The Significance of the Right Hand of Blessing on Ephraim

THE BEST TILL LAST

I have dedicated the major portion of this book to dealing with offences, forgiveness and forgetting. But this last point is truly the best. For when we realise those offences and painful situations of life are also the great opportunities that God uses for our personal development, maturity and for his glory, then we can exercise faith in the purposes of God in our difficulties and offences. The Apostle Peter explains this clearly when he writes… *"In this you greatly rejoice, though now for a little while you may have had to suffer grief in all kinds of trails. These have come so that your faith of greater worth than gold, which perishes even though refined by fire may prove genuine and may result in praise, glory and honour when Christ is revealed"* (1 Peter 1: 6-7). This principle was clearly God's preparation for Joseph and his destiny. He summed up his Theology of life when he said to his brothers – *"you intended to harm me, but God intended it for good to accomplish what is now being done, the saving of many lives"* (Genesis 50:20). When we realise that God wants to use those tough times and offences in order we may "save many lives" of those who go through similar difficult times. It should provide us with the faith to confront those offences with a positive attitude of anticipating that God is at work in our life, perfecting us for His glory and to sharpen our effectiveness for His purposes. For who can effectively minister to a person going through a divorce, than a person who has already been through a divorce, who has walked the walk

> It's so easy to react negatively to offences and miss God's preparation in our life for greater things.

and moved on with their life? Who can effectively walk a person through a serious illness better than those who walked that path and know the victory in Christ? Who can minister to a person suffering from depression better than someone who has walked that dark path and has known the reality of Christ walking with them? Who can share the grief and loss of a loved one better than someone who has known such a loss? Who can best share about dealing with offences, hurts, disappointments and conflicts with church leaders better than someone who has faced those same hurts and overcome them?

I am not suggesting that we no longer need professional counsellors, but I am suggesting there is a wonderful healing potential in the body of Christ that sits dormant because we have not developed the skill of turning our offences and hurts into double blessings and ministry opportunities towards others. We often see only the offences instead of God's ultimate purpose in the offence. It's so easy to react negatively to offences and miss God's preparation in our life for greater things. We must realise we are not a victim, but like Joseph, we are men and women of destiny that believe our times are in His hands and under His control, and for His glory. And like Joseph we will remain faithful to one of God's higher purpose in our life the – "Saving of many lives."

I am endeavouring to apply theological sense of the tough times of life. I am persuaded that if I remove the God factor from my life, I do become a victim of fate, bad luck or chance. That would remove the providential factor of God's influence and leave me exposed to chance. I choose to believe in a loving personal God who is deeply interested in all aspects of my life, that my life is not accidental and my faith in the Almighty provides meaning to life's big question and my purpose for being on this planet.

The realisation of an Ephraim can elevate us from a Manasseh mentality of limiting God's grace only to enabling us to deal with and forget the past hurts. But Ephraim reminds us of God's higher purpose and challenges my faith to see God's higher purpose and to double His blessing on us in the land of suffering. Therefore we can anticipate opportunities to minister into the lives of others. May I suggest that requires looking around you for opportunities to minister to those who are suffering because of hurts and offences, with the intent of imparting the strength God has given you, into their life? I encourage you to desire and pray for a double blessing upon your life and ministry, so like Joseph you may bring deliverance to others, and Glory to God.

Manasseh represents forgetting and that is a blessing and of enormous benefit, but it is restricted to me and my personal world. To a large degree it can be a passive experience in terms of not flowing out and influencing others.

Ephraim however represents a blessing birthed out of the hard times that can become a double blessing to you and through you to others. This Nation needs a gracing of Ephraim ministries, that is, ordinary men and women whom God anoints in providing a ministry of pouring in the oil and wine that brings healing, restoration and freedom to the many who have been bashed by the calamities of life.

I encourage you to believe for an Ephraim of double blessing in your life and ministry, an increase in every area of your life. A double influence in the lives of others, your double opportunity to witness and seeing a double in the number of converts; an increase and double blessing on your health, relationships, family, finances, in joy and happiness and a double increase of the spirit of wisdom, revelation and compassion of Christ.

For the story of Joseph is about God's overwhelming faithfulness and blessing in so many areas of his life. It

> It's time to press ahead and turn offences and tragedies into divine opportunities!

is a story of understanding doing life God's way, living under the principles of his kingdom in such areas as forgiveness, forgetting and fruitfulness. This opens the doors of opportunities for spiritual, emotional, mental and physical blessing and wholeness.

IN SUMMARY

1. Offences are unavoidable and are a fact of life.
2. Forgiveness is the starting point to recovery from offences.
3. God can enable us to forgive and forget our offences by his abundant grace.
4. Forgiveness and forgetfulness are the pathway to fruitfulness.
5. Fruitfulness makes sense of life's offences, trials and testing.

It's time to press ahead and turn offences and tragedies into divine opportunities!

About the Author

Pastor John Lewis

John was the Senior Pastor of a large Pentecostal Church in Everton Park Brisbane Australia for 31 years. During that time he established a Bible College and a Christian School and planted a number of churches. He was the State President, the National Vice President and Chairman of the National Bible College for the A.C.C. (AOG).

John has a passion for missions and in particular the training of Pastors, supporting orphanages and church planting in other nations.

John has been married to his wife Val for 52 years; they have 4 adult children and 9 grandchildren.

John and Val are presently working part time for the State of Queensland and Northern Territory A.C.C., with the designated responsibility of Pastoral Care and Church Consultant. They often travel out-back in their mobile home encouraging the Pastors, meeting with church Boards, preaching and conducting Seminars.

They regularly mentor over 30 Pastors in their home.

John and Val consider being in the ministry a joyful privilege.